THE Saints CHRONICLES

Collection 5

SOPHIA INSTITUTE PRESS
Manchester, NH

PIRITUAL
XERCISES

SOPHIA
INSTITUTE PRESS

Printed in the United States of America.

Sophia Institute Press®
Box 5284, Manchester, NH 03108
1-800-888-9344

www.SophiaInstitute.com
Sophia Institute Press® is a registered trademark of Sophia Institute.

Names, persons, places, and incidents featured in this publication are based on historical fact but have been subject to author and artist discretion for dramatic purposes. All text, except when specifically cited, has been written by the author, not to be mistaken for actual historical documentation.

The Saints Chronicles Collection 1, ISBN: 9781622826742
The Saints Chronicles Collection 2, ISBN: 9781622826766
The Saints Chronicles Collection 3, ISBN: 9781622826797
The Saints Chronicles Collection 4, ISBN: 9781622826803
The Saints Chronicles Collection 5, ISBN: 9781644133149

Library of Congress Cataloging-in-Publication Data

Title: The saints chronicles. Collection 1. Saint Patrick, Saint Jerome Emiliani, Saint Elizabeth Ann Seton, Saint Henry Morse, Saint Joan of Arc.
Description: Manchester, NH : Sophia Institute Press, [2018]
Identifiers: LCCN 2018038952 | ISBN 9781622826742 (pbk. : alk. paper)
Subjects: LCSH: Christian saints–Biography–Comic books, strips, etc. | Christian martyrs–Biography–Comic books, strips, etc. | Catholics–Biography–Comic books, strips, etc. | Patrick, Saint, 373?-463? –Comic books, strips, etc. | Jerome Emiliani, Saint, 1486-1537 –Comic books, strips, etc. | Seton, Elizabeth Ann, Saint, 1774-1821 –Comic books, strips, etc. | Morse, Henry, Saint, 1595-1645 –Comic books, strips, etc. | Joan, of Arc, Saint, 1412-1431 –Comic books, strips, etc. | Graphic novels.
Classification: LCC BX4655.3 .S255 2018 | DDC 282.092/2 [B] –dc23
LC record available at https://lccn.loc.gov/2018038952

3rd printing

THE Saints CHRONICLES

Collection 5

What books have inspired you to think differently about your life?

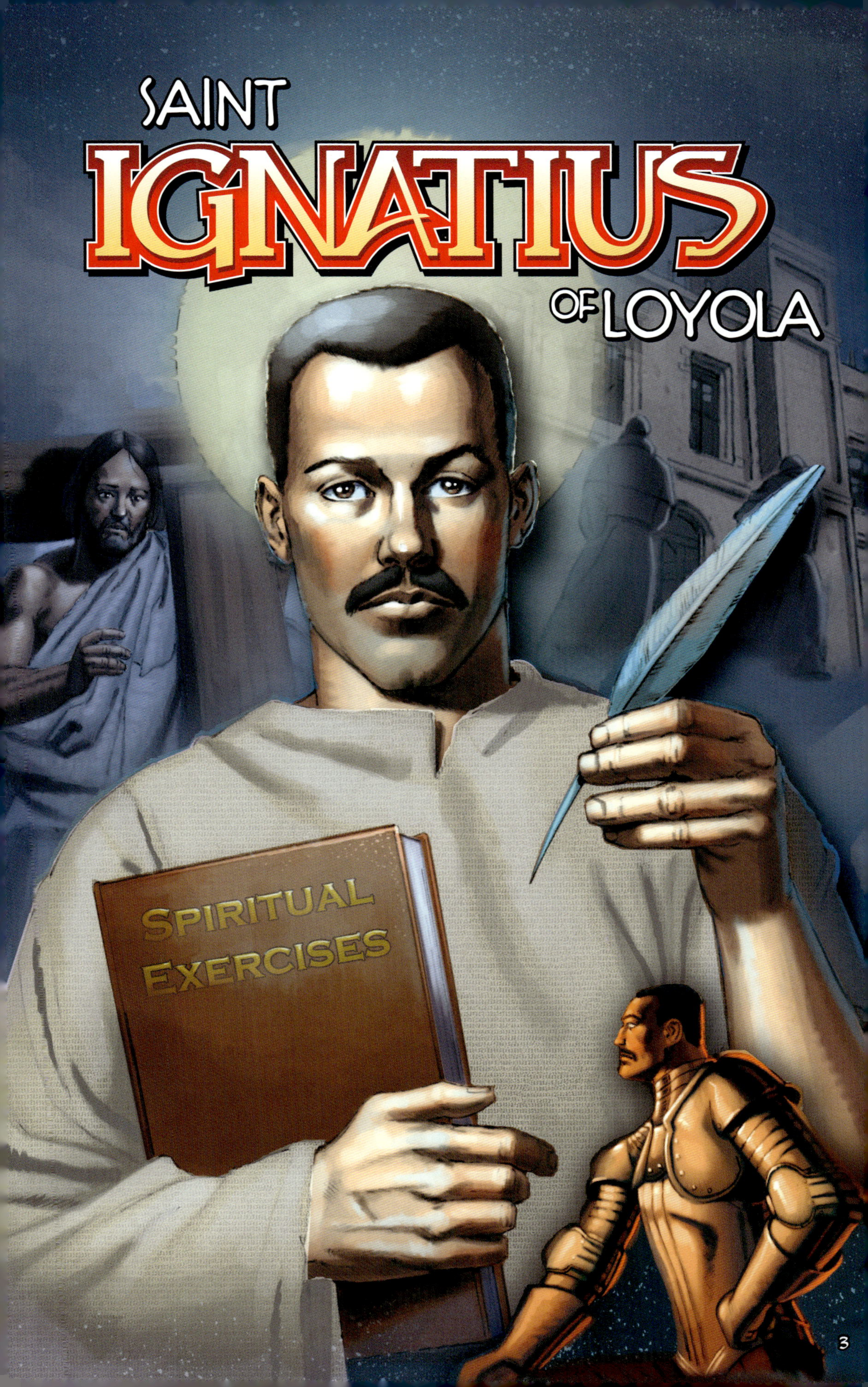
SAINT
IGNATIUS
OF LOYOLA
SPIRITUAL
EXERCISES

SAINT IGNATIUS OF LOYOLA

IGNATIUS OF LOYOLA IS BEST KNOWN FOR FOUNDING THE SOCIETY OF JESUS -- MORE COMMONLY KNOWN AS THE ***JESUITS*** -- TO PROMOTE THE SPREAD OF ***CATHOLICISM*** IN EUROPE. BUT THE COMPLETE STORY IS MUCH MORE COMPLEX, AND REVEALS A COMPELLING TALE OF FINDING ***FAITH*** AND ***PURPOSE*** IN LIFE.

THOUGH BORN AND RAISED IN A ***CHRISTIAN*** LAND, IGNATIUS DID NOT GROW UP A PARTICULARLY RELIGIOUS MAN. IT WAS ONLY AT THE AGE OF ***THIRTY,*** WHEN CIRCUMSTANCE FORCED A ***TREMENDOUS CHANGE*** IN HIS LIFE, THAT HE WAS ***REINTRODUCED*** TO THE FAITH OF HIS PARENTS. THROUGHOUT THIS CHANGE, IGNATIUS FELT THE VERY HUMAN EMOTIONS OF ***DOUBT*** AND ***UNCERTAINTY,*** BOTH ABOUT HIS CHOICE OF A ***NEW LIFE*** AND THE ***WAY*** HE WOULD ***PURSUE*** THAT CHOICE.

IGNATIUS FACED HIS DOUBTS AND STRENGTHENED HIS FAITH THROUGH THE ***TWIN PILLARS*** OF ***OBEDIENCE*** AND ***EDUCATION***. HE SOUGHT TO LEARN FROM LIFE AND FROM FORMAL SCHOOLING TO BUILD HIS FAITH AND ENABLE HIM ***TO MINISTER*** TO THE PEOPLE AROUND HIM. IGNATIUS BACKED THIS EDUCATION WITH ***UNWAVERING OBEDIENCE*** TO THE CHURCH AND HER LEADERS, EVEN DURING THOSE TIMES WHEN THEY ***DISAGREED***.

THOUGH THE SOCIETY OF JESUS WAS NOT ORIGINALLY FOUNDED TO FIGHT PROTESTANTISM, AND IGNATIUS WAS ONLY ONE OF ITS FOUNDERS, HE TRULY WAS AND STILL REMAINS THE HEART AND SOUL OF THE JESUITS AND LED THE WAY IN ***DEFENDING THE CHURCH***. HIS LIFE STORY IS A ***CLEAR EXAMPLE*** FOR ANYONE WHO WANTS TO ***FOLLOW*** AND ***DEVELOP HIS/HER FAITH,*** FOR IN HIS DOUBTS WE CAN SEE THAT WE CAN BE FAITHFUL DESPITE IT ALL, AND IN HIS DEVOTION TO EDUCATION AND OBEDIENCE, WE SEE THE WAY TO ***BUILDING*** OUR FAITH ***IN SPITE OF OUR FLAWS.***

EDUCATION OBEDIENCE

- PRODUCER -	- DANIEL BURTON -
- EDITOR -	- KIMBERLY BLACK -
- STORY -	- ALEXANDER SHEARER -
- ART -	- JASON MILLET -
- LETTERS -	- KEITH BAHRENBURG -
- DESIGNS -	- DANIEL BURTON -

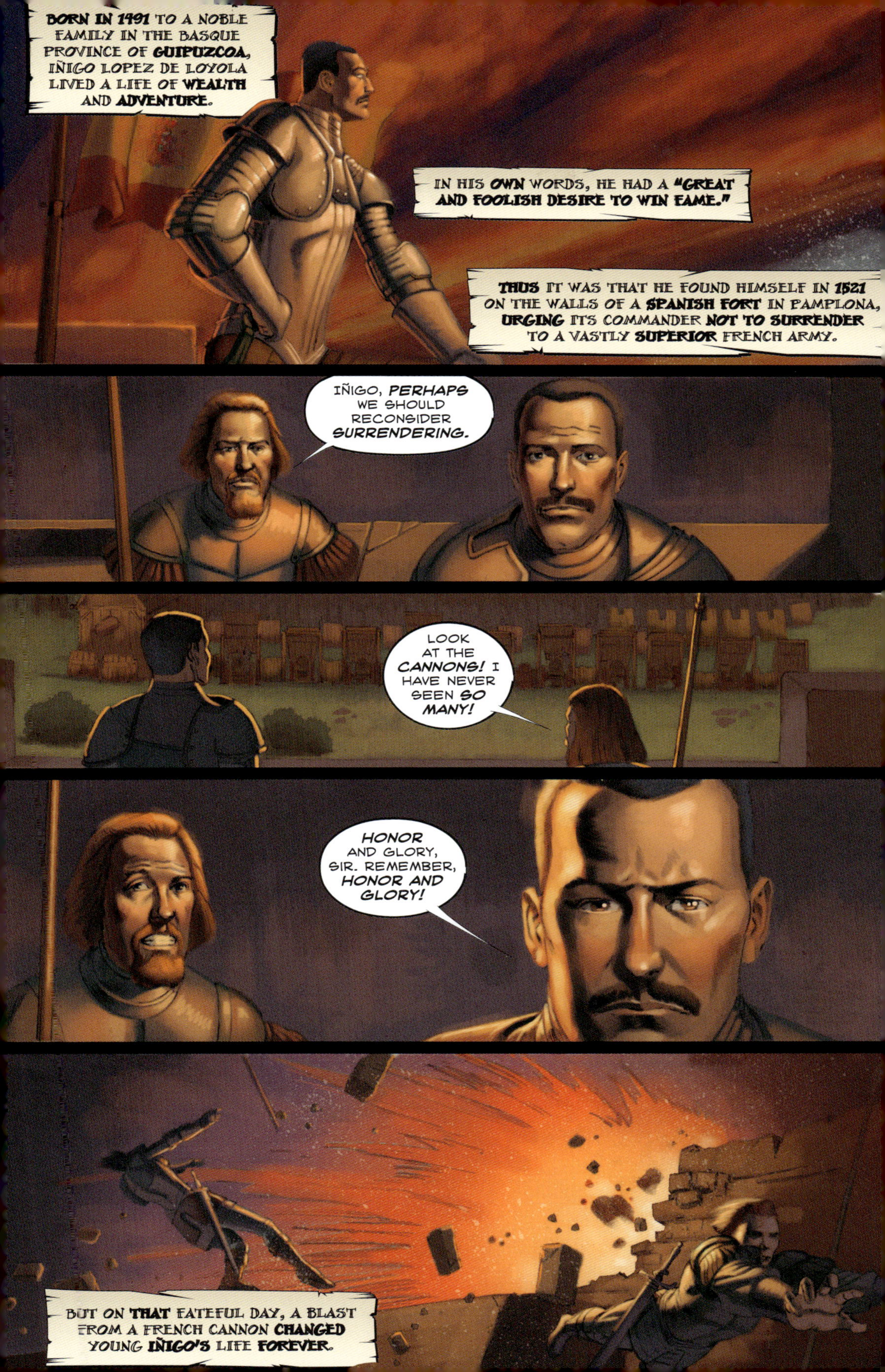
BORN IN 1491 TO A NOBLE FAMILY IN THE BASQUE PROVINCE OF GUIPUZCOA, IÑIGO LOPEZ DE LOYOLA LIVED A LIFE OF WEALTH AND ADVENTURE.
IN HIS OWN WORDS, HE HAD A "GREAT AND FOOLISH DESIRE TO WIN FAME."
THUS IT WAS THAT HE FOUND HIMSELF IN 1521 ON THE WALLS OF A SPANISH FORT IN PAMPLONA, URGING ITS COMMANDER NOT TO SURRENDER TO A VASTLY SUPERIOR FRENCH ARMY.
IÑIGO, PERHAPS WE SHOULD RECONSIDER SURRENDERING.
LOOK AT THE CANNONS! I HAVE NEVER SEEN SO MANY!
HONOR AND GLORY, SIR. REMEMBER, HONOR AND GLORY!
BUT ON THAT FATEFUL DAY, A BLAST FROM A FRENCH CANNON CHANGED YOUNG IÑIGO'S LIFE FOREVER.

THOUGH THEY WERE ENEMIES, THE FRENCH SOLDIERS WERE SO IMPRESSED WITH HIS BRAVERY THAT THEY CARRIED IÑIGO ALL THE WAY TO HIS HOME IN LOYOLA.
AND, AGAINST ALL ODDS, IÑIGO RECOVERED ON THE FEAST DAY OF SAINTS PETER AND PAUL.
YOUR RECOVERY IS TRULY REMARKABLE, IÑIGO, BUT I AM AFRAID YOUR LEG WILL NEVER COMPLETELY HEAL.
WE'LL JUST HAVE TO SEE ABOUT THAT! I HAVE A LIFE TO RETURN TO, ONCE I AM WELL. THE COURTS EAGERLY AWAIT MY RETURN!
TSK TSK
YOUNG MAN -- I AM ABOUT TO LOSE MY MIND FROM ALL THIS RESTING.
PLEASE, BRING ME SOMETHING TO READ. BOOKS -- KNIGHTLY ADVENTURES. SOMETHING TO TAKE ME AWAY FROM THIS BOREDOM!
I'LL SEE WHAT I CAN DO, SIR.
I'M SORRY SIR, BUT THESE ARE THE ONLY BOOKS IN THE HOUSEHOLD.
THIS BOOK ON THE LIFE OF OUR SAVIOR, AND ANOTHER ON THE LIVES OF THE SAINTS, THE "GOLDEN LEGEND."
THAT'S FINE. I'LL MAKE DO WITH THESE.
TO HIS CREDIT, IÑIGO READ THE BOOKS, AND SO BEGAN HIS JOURNEY TO BECOME THE MAN WE NOW KNOW AS SAINT IGNATIUS OF LOYOLA, FOUNDER OF THE SOCIETY OF JESUS.

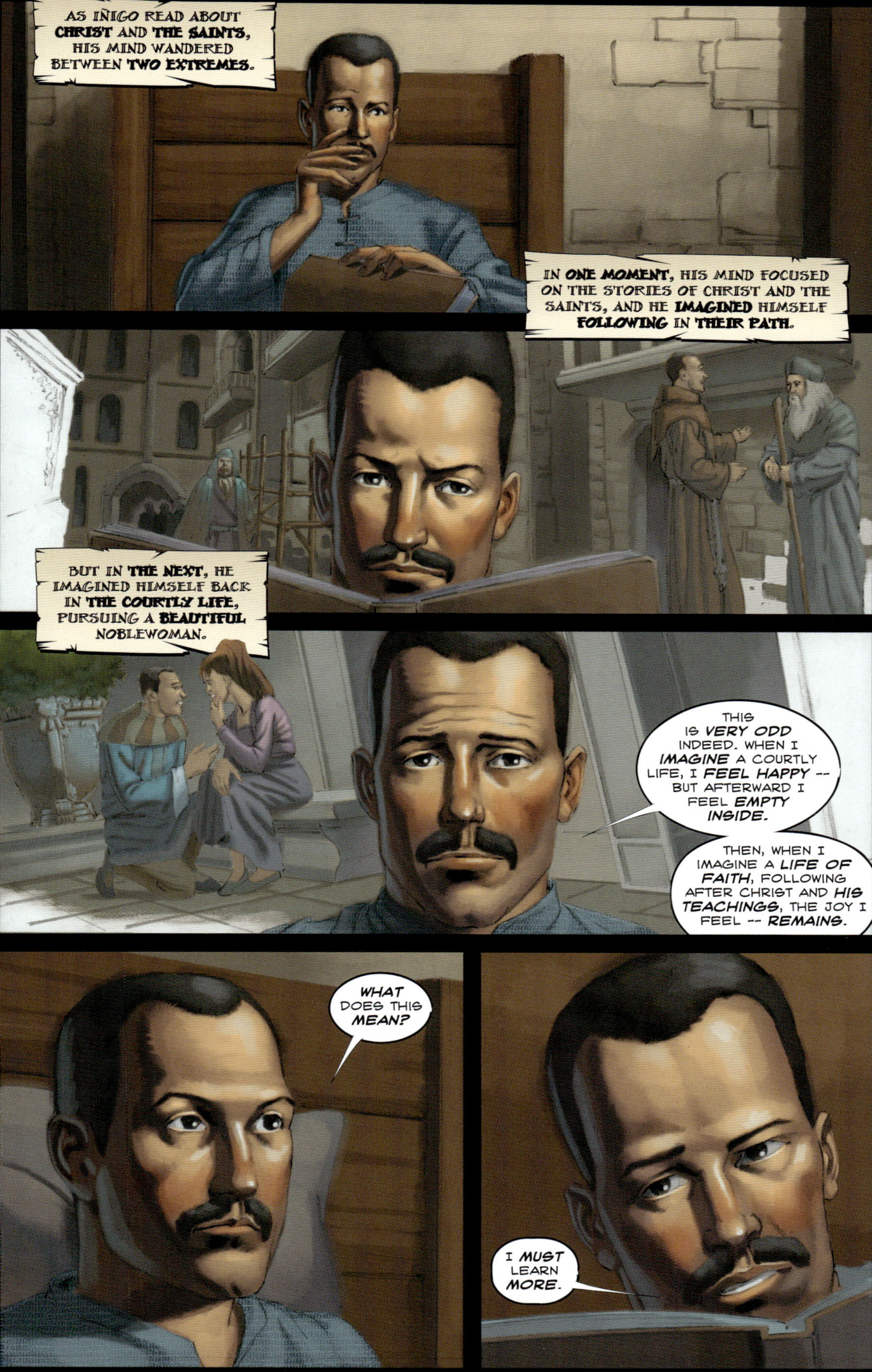

AS IÑIGO READ ABOUT CHRIST AND THE SAINTS, HIS MIND WANDERED BETWEEN TWO EXTREMES.
IN ONE MOMENT, HIS MIND FOCUSED ON THE STORIES OF CHRIST AND THE SAINTS, AND HE IMAGINED HIMSELF FOLLOWING IN THEIR PATH.
BUT IN THE NEXT, HE IMAGINED HIMSELF BACK IN THE COURTLY LIFE, PURSUING A BEAUTIFUL NOBLEWOMAN.
THIS IS VERY ODD INDEED. WHEN I IMAGINE A COURTLY LIFE, I FEEL HAPPY -- BUT AFTERWARD I FEEL EMPTY INSIDE.
THEN, WHEN I IMAGINE A LIFE OF FAITH, FOLLOWING AFTER CHRIST AND HIS TEACHINGS, THE JOY I FEEL -- REMAINS.
WHAT DOES THIS MEAN?
I MUST LEARN MORE.

ON THAT NIGHT, IÑIGO RECEIVED THE FIRST OF MANY VISIONS HE WOULD HAVE IN HIS LIFE --
-- AND IN THAT VERY MOMENT, IÑIGO FELT HIS SPIRIT HAD FINALLY BEEN CLEANSED OF THE LIFE HE'D LED BEFORE.
I KNOW WHAT I MUST DO.
I MUST GO TO JERUSALEM.
SOON AFTER HIS VISION, IÑIGO LEFT HIS HOME AND TRAVELED TO MONTSERRAT, WHERE HE SPENT TIME WRITING HIS CONFESSION, DESCRIBING THE LIFE HE WAS LEAVING BEHIND. HE ALSO WROTE MATERIAL FOR WHAT WOULD BECOME HIS BOOK, "SPIRITUAL EXERCISES."

AS HE HAD ONCE CARED SO MUCH ABOUT HIS LOOKS, IÑIGO DECIDED TO STOP CUTTING HIS HAIR.
HE ALSO GAVE UP MEAT FOR QUITE A WHILE AND PRACTICED THE DISCIPLINE OF FASTING FOR DAYS ON END.
BUT STILL, HE HAD HIS DOUBTS.
SOME DAYS I AM HAPPY BEYOND BELIEF, YET ON OTHERS, NOTHING CAN LIFT MY MOOD.
WHAT NEW LIFE IS THIS THAT I AM NOW BEGINNING?
I MUST SPEND TIME IN PRAYER. THE LORD WILL BE FAITHFUL AND HIS ANSWERS WILL FIND ME.
EACH NIGHT IÑIGO LAY AWAKE, BOMBARDED WITH NEW IDEAS THAT FELT LIKE ENLIGHTENMENT. BUT, AS USUAL -- HE HAD HIS DOUBTS ...
I SET ASIDE ALMOST MY ENTIRE DAY FOR CONVERSATION WITH YOU, LORD. WHY THEN DO YOU COME TO ME DURING THESE FEW LATE HOURS I HAVE GIVEN MYSELF TO SLEEP?
AFTER MUCH THOUGHT, HE CONCLUDED THAT THESE NIGHTLY DISTRACTIONS WERE TEMPTATIONS, AND NOT FROM GOD. THUS HE IGNORED THEM, INSTEAD SLEEPING SO THAT HE COULD BETTER SERVE GOD DURING HIS WAKING HOURS.
A YEAR QUICKLY PASSED ...
AFTER ALL THIS TIME, YOU'RE CUTTING YOUR HAIR?
IN THE LAST YEAR, I HAVE COME TO UNDERSTAND THE DELICATE BALANCE BETWEEN DEVOTION AND EXCESS.
MY TIME FOR SITTING ALONE AND CONTEMPLATING THE FAITH IS OVER.

EARLY IN 1523, IÑIGO FINALLY SET OUT TOWARD JERUSALEM. AS HE WENT, MANY TRIED TO CONVINCE HIM TO PROCEED CAUTIOUSLY.
YOU JUST CAN'T MAKE THIS KIND OF TRIP ALONE. IT'S VERY DANGEROUS AND YOU DON'T EVEN SPEAK A WORD OF LATIN OR ITALIAN. HOW DO YOU EXPECT TO GET ON A SHIP IN VENICE ANYWAY?
HE'S RIGHT! YOU SHOULD GO WITH SOMEONE LIKE DIEGO DE LA FUENTE.
YES. DIEGO IS A GOOD MAN, AND HE SPEAKS EXCELLENT ITALIAN.
I DO APPRECIATE YOUR CONCERN, FRIENDS.
BUT EVEN IF THE MAN YOU NAMED WERE THE BROTHER OF THE DUKE OF CARDONA HIMSELF, I WOULD NOT GO IN HIS COMPANY.
BUT WHY?
I WISH TO PRACTICE THE VIRTUES OF
CHARITY,
FAITH,
AND
HOPE
ON THIS JOURNEY.
IF I HAD A COMPANION, HE WOULD HELP ME WHEN I GREW HUNGRY OR LIFT ME UP IF I FELL. I MUST INSTEAD PLACE MY TRUST AND HOPE IN GOD ALONE.
IÑIGO SOON ARRIVED IN JERUSALEM THAT SEPTEMBER. HE WAS FILLED WITH JOY, AND WENT TO FULFILL THE SECOND PART OF HIS PLAN -- TO HELP SOULS IN THE HOLY CITY.

HOWEVER, THE LOCAL CLERGY HAD OTHER IDEAS.
I DO APPRECIATE YOUR GOOD INTENTIONS, IÑIGO.
BUT THESE ARE ROUGH TIMES, AND MANY OTHERS WITH THESE SAME INTENTIONS HAVE BEEN KILLED, OR CAPTURED AND RANSOMED BACK TO US.
I'M AFRAID YOU MUST RETURN HOME.
I AM RESOLVED TO CARRY OUT MY PURPOSE IN JERUSALEM, SIR.
UNLESS IT IS SOMEHOW A SIN, I WILL NOT BE SCARED OFF BY TALES OF KIDNAPPING AND DEATH.
IÑIGO, THE HOLY SEE HAS GIVEN US THE AUTHORITY TO HAVE ANYONE STAY, OR LEAVE, AS WE JUDGE IS BEST.
I WOULD BE GLAD TO SHOW YOU THE PAPERS GIVING US THIS POWER.
THERE IS NO NEED FOR THAT.
I WILL RETURN HOME AS SOON AS I CAN.
IN LEAVING JERUSALEM, IÑIGO PROMINENTLY DISPLAYED HIS GREAT OBEDIENCE TO THE CHURCH NO MATTER THE PRICE. THIS OBEDIENCE WOULD ONE DAY BECOME A DEFINING ELEMENT OF THE SOCIETY OF JESUS.

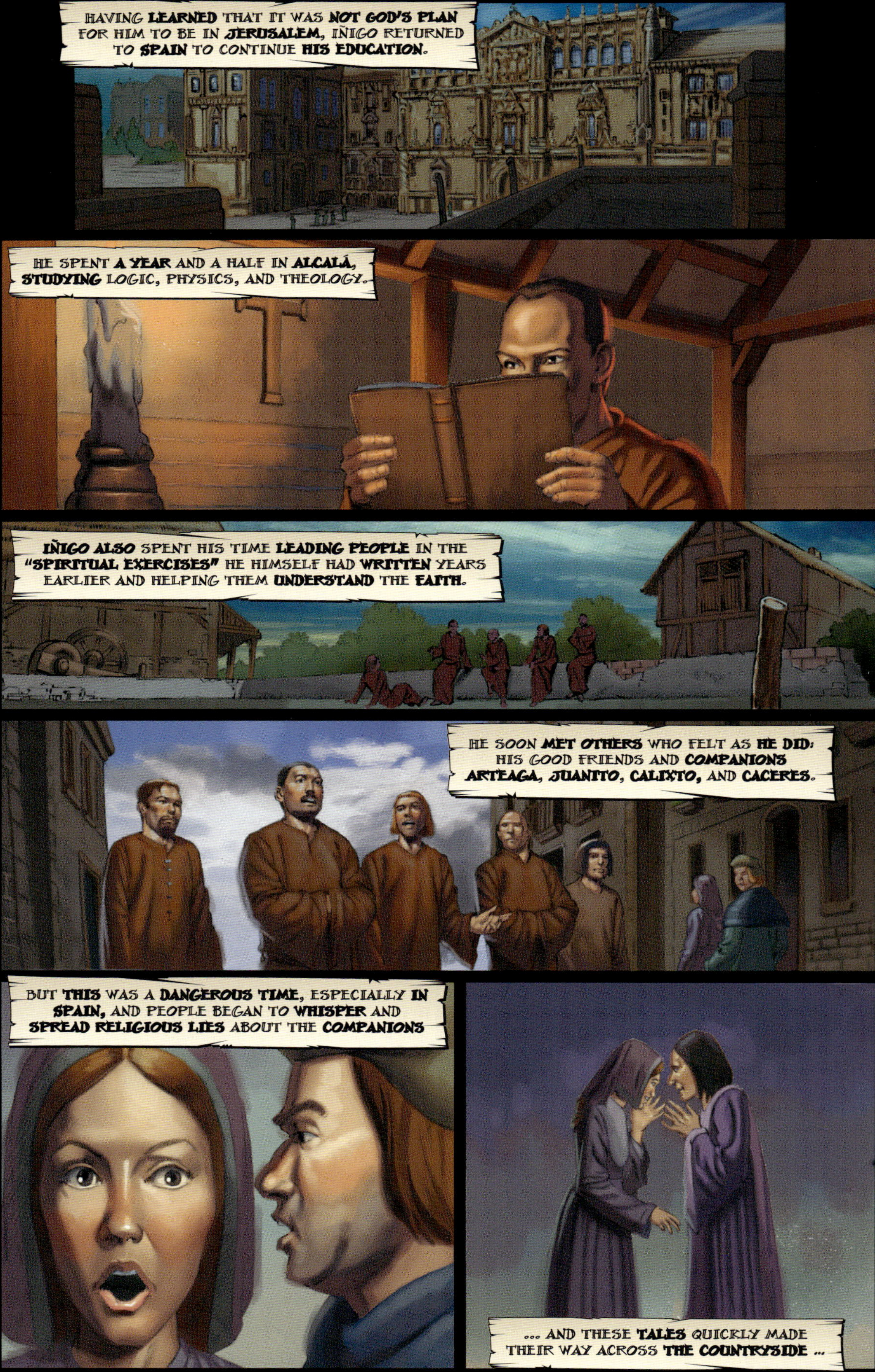
HAVING LEARNED THAT IT WAS NOT GOD'S PLAN FOR HIM TO BE IN JERUSALEM, IÑIGO RETURNED TO SPAIN TO CONTINUE HIS EDUCATION.
HE SPENT A YEAR AND A HALF IN ALCALÁ, STUDYING LOGIC, PHYSICS, AND THEOLOGY.
IÑIGO ALSO SPENT HIS TIME LEADING PEOPLE IN THE "SPIRITUAL EXERCISES" HE HIMSELF HAD WRITTEN YEARS EARLIER AND HELPING THEM UNDERSTAND THE FAITH.
HE SOON MET OTHERS WHO FELT AS HE DID: HIS GOOD FRIENDS AND COMPANIONS ARTEAGA, JUANITO, CALIXTO, AND CACERES.
BUT THIS WAS A DANGEROUS TIME, ESPECIALLY IN SPAIN, AND PEOPLE BEGAN TO WHISPER AND SPREAD RELIGIOUS LIES ABOUT THE COMPANIONS
... AND THESE TALES QUICKLY MADE THEIR WAY ACROSS THE COUNTRYSIDE ...

... EVENTUALLY REACHING THE EARS OF THOSE LEADING THE INQUISITION.
NO.
IÑIGO! YOU ARE IN DANGER!
WHAT IS IT, DON DIEGO?
THE INQUISITORS HAVE COME TO ALCALÁ AND THEY ARE SAYING TERRIBLE THINGS ABOUT YOUR MINISTRY HERE.
THEY ARE CALLING YOU "WEARER OF SACKCLOTH" AND "ILLUMINATI," AS IF YOU BELONGED TO A HERETIC SECT!
IÑIGO -- THEY'RE GOING TO KILL YOU.
DON'T WORRY, FRIEND. GOD GUIDES US IN THIS, AS HE DOES IN ALL THINGS.
INDEED IÑIGO WAS RIGHT: THE INQUISITORS CHOSE TO LEAVE THE MATTER TO LOCAL CHURCH OFFICIALS ...
... WHO REACHED THE CURIOUS CONCLUSION THAT THE COMPANIONS COULD CONTINUE TO TEACH, AS LONG AS THEY DYED THEIR ROBES DIFFERENT COLORS.

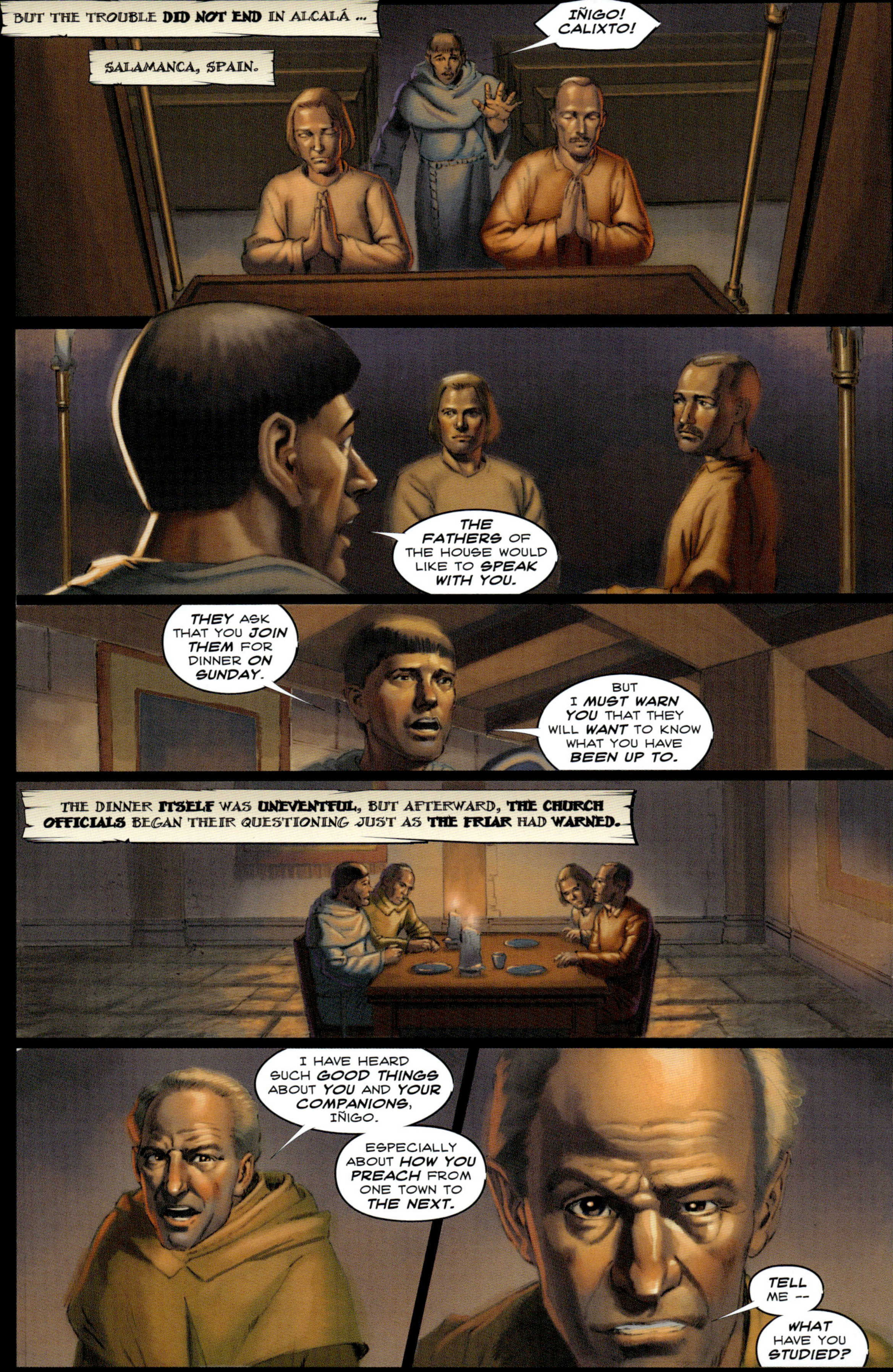
BUT THE TROUBLE DID NOT END IN ALCALÁ ...
SALAMANCA, SPAIN.
IÑIGO! CALIXTO!
THE FATHERS OF THE HOUSE WOULD LIKE TO SPEAK WITH YOU.
THEY ASK THAT YOU JOIN THEM FOR DINNER ON SUNDAY.
BUT I MUST WARN YOU THAT THEY WILL WANT TO KNOW WHAT YOU HAVE BEEN UP TO.
THE DINNER ITSELF WAS UNEVENTFUL, BUT AFTERWARD, THE CHURCH OFFICIALS BEGAN THEIR QUESTIONING JUST AS THE FRIAR HAD WARNED.
I HAVE HEARD SUCH GOOD THINGS ABOUT YOU AND YOUR COMPANIONS, IÑIGO.
ESPECIALLY ABOUT HOW YOU PREACH FROM ONE TOWN TO THE NEXT.
TELL ME --
WHAT HAVE YOU STUDIED?

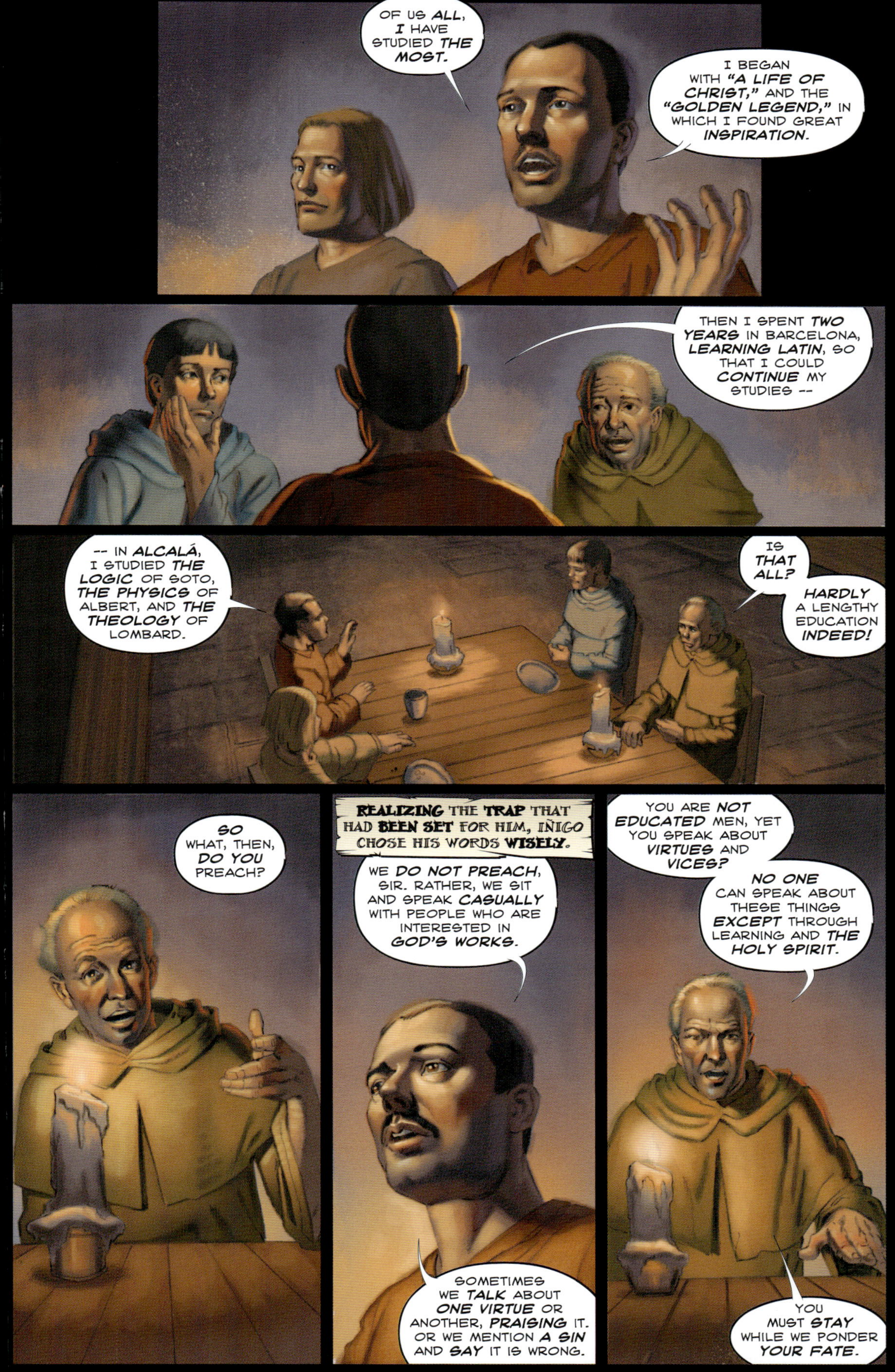
OF US ALL, I HAVE STUDIED THE MOST.
I BEGAN WITH "A LIFE OF CHRIST," AND THE "GOLDEN LEGEND," IN WHICH I FOUND GREAT INSPIRATION.
THEN I SPENT TWO YEARS IN BARCELONA, LEARNING LATIN, SO THAT I COULD CONTINUE MY STUDIES --
-- IN ALCALÁ, I STUDIED THE LOGIC OF SOTO, THE PHYSICS OF ALBERT, AND THE THEOLOGY OF LOMBARD.
IS THAT ALL?
HARDLY A LENGTHY EDUCATION INDEED!
SO WHAT, THEN, DO YOU PREACH?
REALIZING THE TRAP THAT HAD BEEN SET FOR HIM, IÑIGO CHOSE HIS WORDS WISELY.
WE DO NOT PREACH, SIR. RATHER, WE SIT AND SPEAK CASUALLY WITH PEOPLE WHO ARE INTERESTED IN GOD'S WORKS.
SOMETIMES WE TALK ABOUT ONE VIRTUE OR ANOTHER, PRAISING IT. OR WE MENTION A SIN AND SAY IT IS WRONG.
YOU ARE NOT EDUCATED MEN, YET YOU SPEAK ABOUT VIRTUES AND VICES?
NO ONE CAN SPEAK ABOUT THESE THINGS EXCEPT THROUGH LEARNING AND THE HOLY SPIRIT.
YOU MUST STAY WHILE WE PONDER YOUR FATE.

IÑIGO AND CALIXTO WERE JAILED WHILE THEIR FATE WAS DETERMINED. THEY SPENT THEIR FIRST NIGHT IN AN EMPTY PRISON CELL, CHAINED TOGETHER.
IT'S TERRIBLE THAT THEY HAVE YOU TWO IN HERE, IÑIGO.
FEAR NOT; GOD WATCHES OVER US.
HERE YOU GO, CALIXTO. WE BROUGHT THESE MATS SO YOU WON'T HAVE TO SLEEP ON THE FLOOR.
THANK YOU. YOUR PRESENCE IS A BLESSING.
A SCHOLAR CAME BY TO QUESTION IÑIGO AND CALIXTO.
HE ALSO TOOK THE NOTES IÑIGO HAD BEEN WORKING ON, WHICH WOULD ONE DAY BECOME HIS FAMOUS "SPIRITUAL EXERCISES."
SOON AFTER THEIR DETENTION, IÑIGO AND CALIXTO WELCOMED THEIR COMPANIONS CACERES AND ARTEAGA TO THEIR HOLDING CELL.
WE COULDN'T LET YOU LANGUISH IN PRISON WITHOUT US!
AFTER MANY WEEKS, IÑIGO AND HIS FRIENDS WERE BROUGHT BEFORE THE AUTHORITIES ON RELIGIOUS MATTERS.
THEY WERE QUESTIONED EXTENSIVELY AND SPOKE HONESTLY ABOUT THEIR LEARNING AND TEACHING.
IN THE END, THE JUDGES MADE AN INTERESTING DECISION.
WE HAVE FOUND NO ERROR IN YOUR LIVES OR IN YOUR TEACHINGS. YOU MAY GO ON TEACHING DOCTRINE AND SPEAKING ABOUT GOD. BUT YOU MAY NOT TEACH ABOUT WHAT IS OR IS NOT SINFUL UNTIL YOU HAVE ALL HAD ANOTHER FOUR YEARS OF EDUCATION.

COMMANDED BY THE JUDGES TO LEARN MORE BEFORE TEACHING, IÑIGO WENT TO PARIS TO FURTHER HIS EDUCATION IN THEOLOGY. THERE HE ALSO CHANGED HIS NAME FROM IÑIGO TO IGNATIUS.
HE BENEFITED SO MUCH FROM THE ORGANIZED WAY TEACHING WAS DONE IN PARIS THAT HE LATER INSISTED THAT MEMBERS OF THE SOCIETY OF JESUS LEARN BY THE SAME METHOD.
ON COMPLETING THEIR EDUCATION, IGNATIUS AND SIX OF HIS COMPANIONS CAME TOGETHER TO MAKE A VOW FOR THEIR FUTURE.
IT'S AGREED, THEN. IN A YEAR WE WILL ALL GO TO VENICE, AND FROM THERE TO JERUSALEM, TO SPEND THE REST OF OUR LIVES FOR THE GOOD OF THOSE THERE.
IF WE CANNOT GO TO JERUSALEM, THEN WE WILL GO TO ROME AND PUT OURSELVES AT THE POPE'S SERVICE.
JERUSALEM AND ROME!
IGNATIUS WAS FORTY-THREE WHEN HE COMPLETED HIS EDUCATION AND TOOK THIS VOW.
ONCE THEY REACHED VENICE, THE COMPANIONS WAITED AND WAITED FOR A CHANCE TO GO TO JERUSALEM, BUT THERE WAS A PROBLEM ...
I CAN'T TAKE YOU THERE -- NO ONE CAN. THE TURKS AREN'T HAPPY WITH US RIGHT NOW, SO NO SHIPS, NO PASSENGERS --
-- NO JERUSALEM.
WITH THIS NEWS, THE COMPANIONS SPENT THEIR DAYS PREACHING TO THE CITIZENS OF VENICE AND WAITING FOR TRAVEL TO THE HOLY LAND TO RESUME.
BUT EACH TIME THEY CHECKED, THE STORY WAS THE SAME.
THE ANSWER IS STILL "NO." THEY'RE JUST NOT LETTING US INTO THEIR PORTS.
... AND SO IT WENT, MONTH AFTER MONTH, UNTIL ...
OUR YEAR HAS PASSED, IGNATIUS.
WE WILL SEE EACH OTHER IN ROME, THEN.

TOGETHER WITH TWO OF HIS COMPANIONS, IGNATIUS MADE HIS WAY FROM VENICE TO ROME.
IF SOMEONE ASKS WHO WE ARE AS WE TRAVEL, LET US SAY WE ARE "THE COMPANY OF JESUS," FOR WE ARE UNITED TO FIGHT FALSEHOOD UNDER THE STANDARD OF CHRIST.
THEN, DURING A PAUSE FOR PRAYER IN LA STORTA...
... IGNATIUS HAD ANOTHER VISION.
I will favor you at Rome.
THIS IS QUITE A VISION, BUT WHAT DOES IT MEAN?
DOES THIS MEAN ROME WILL BE GOOD FOR ME, OR WILL I BE PERSECUTED AS CHRIST WAS?
EITHER WAY, I WILL LIVE AS GOD DESIRES. I WILL CONTINUE ON, TO ROME.

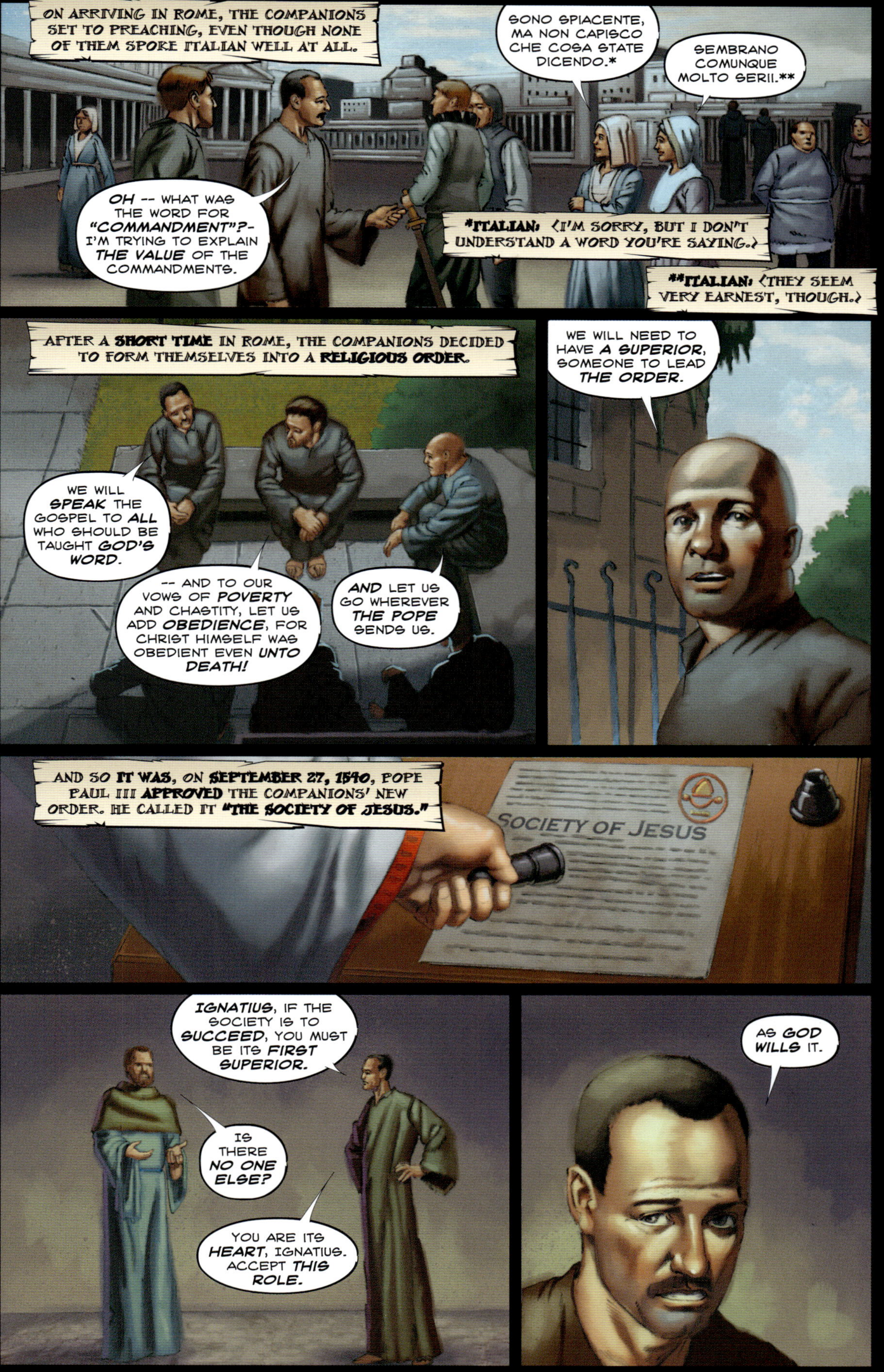
ON ARRIVING IN ROME, THE COMPANIONS SET TO PREACHING, EVEN THOUGH NONE OF THEM SPOKE ITALIAN WELL AT ALL.
OH -- WHAT WAS THE WORD FOR "COMMANDMENT"?- I'M TRYING TO EXPLAIN THE VALUE OF THE COMMANDMENTS.
SONO SPIACENTE, MA NON CAPISCO CHE COSA STATE DICENDO.*
SEMBRANO COMUNQUE MOLTO SERII.**
*ITALIAN: <I'M SORRY, BUT I DON'T UNDERSTAND A WORD YOU'RE SAYING.>
**ITALIAN: <THEY SEEM VERY EARNEST, THOUGH.>
AFTER A SHORT TIME IN ROME, THE COMPANIONS DECIDED TO FORM THEMSELVES INTO A RELIGIOUS ORDER.
WE WILL SPEAK THE GOSPEL TO ALL WHO SHOULD BE TAUGHT GOD'S WORD.
-- AND TO OUR VOWS OF POVERTY AND CHASTITY, LET US ADD OBEDIENCE, FOR CHRIST HIMSELF WAS OBEDIENT EVEN UNTO DEATH!
AND LET US GO WHEREVER THE POPE SENDS US.
WE WILL NEED TO HAVE A SUPERIOR, SOMEONE TO LEAD THE ORDER.
AND SO IT WAS, ON SEPTEMBER 27, 1540, POPE PAUL III APPROVED THE COMPANIONS' NEW ORDER. HE CALLED IT "THE SOCIETY OF JESUS."
SOCIETY OF JESUS
IGNATIUS, IF THE SOCIETY IS TO SUCCEED, YOU MUST BE ITS FIRST SUPERIOR.
IS THERE NO ONE ELSE?
YOU ARE ITS HEART, IGNATIUS. ACCEPT THIS ROLE.
AS GOD WILLS IT.

IGNATIUS SPENT THE REST OF HIS LIFE IN ROME, FIRST DEVELOPING THE CONSTITUTIONS OF THE NEW SOCIETY OF JESUS, AND THEN DIRECTING THE ORDER.
NEW MEMBERS OF THE SOCIETY MADE THEIR VOWS AT THE BASILICA OF SAINT-PAUL-OUTSIDE-THE-WALLS.
AS YOU CAN SEE, WE HAVE ESTABLISHED HERE A HOUSE FOR CONVERTS IN THEIR TIME OF INSTRUCTION.
WE STRIVE TO HELP THEM LEARN TO RELY ON GOD IN ALL THINGS.
DON'T YOU FEAR THAT MOST OF THESE CONVERSIONS ARE INSINCERE, AND THE PEOPLE ARE LIKELY TO LEAVE THE FAITH AGAIN?
TO PREVENT EVEN ONE SIN WOULD BE A GREAT BLESSING, NO MATTER THE COST.
FOR THIS REASON, IT IS WORTH IT.

WITH FUNDS FROM FRANCIS BORGIA, IGNATIUS FOUNDED A ROMAN COLLEGE TO TRAIN FUTURE MEMBERS OF THE SOCIETY. THIS MARRED THE COMMITMENT OF THE JESUIT ORDER TO A FIRM EDUCATIONAL FOUNDATION.
THANKS TO YOUR GENEROUS SUPPORT, OUR COLLEGE IS ALMOST READY.
YOU WILL TEACH THEM THE VALUE OF EDUCATION, IGNATIUS.
THEN, "SPIRITUAL EXERCISES," THE BOOK IGNATIUS BEGAN SO LONG AGO, WAS FINALLY PUBLISHED IN 1548 WITH VATICAN APPROVAL.
SPIRITUAL EXERCISES
WITHIN ITS PAGES LAY MEDITATIONS, WRITTEN WITH THE GOAL OF LETTING ITS READERS ...
... MAKE A CHOICE ABOUT A CRISIS OR THE COURSE OF THEIR LIVES, UNBIASED AND SOLELY CONSIDERING WHAT WILL BE BEST FOR THE ONE END FOR WHICH WE WERE ALL CREATED -- THE GLORY OF GOD AND THE PERFECTION OF OUR SOULS.
INDEED, THIS IDEA IS EMBODIED IN THE MOTTO OF OUR SOCIETY:
TO THE GREATER GLORY OF GOD.

DURING THE FIFTEEN YEARS IN WHICH IGNATIUS LED THE SOCIETY, ITS MEMBERSHIP GREW FROM TEN ...
... TO A THOUSAND.
WITH MEMBERS IN EUROPE ...
... SOUTH AMERICA ...
... AND AFRICA.
IT CONTINUES ON, TO THIS DAY.
THERE ARE ALMOST TWENTY THOUSAND MEMBERS OF THE SOCIETY OF JESUS, COMMONLY KNOWN AS JESUITS. THEY FOLLOW IN THE FOOTSTEPS OF IGNATIUS OF LOYOLA, A MAN WHO FOUND HIS FAITH, SOUGHT THE TRUTH, AND SERVED GOD IN ALL HE DID.

A Saint's Journey

1491 -- IÑIGO IS BORN THE YOUNGEST OF EIGHT SONS AND THREE DAUGHTERS IN THE BASQUE PROVINCE OF GUIPUZCOA.

1521 -- BADLY INJURED BY A CANNON SHOT AT THE SIEGE OF PAMPLONA. DURING HIS RECOVERY, HE FIRST FINDS HIS FAITH. HE LATER TAKES THE NAME IGNATIUS.

1523 -- TRAVELS TO JERUSALEM, BUT IS TURNED AWAY BY THE LOCAL CLERGY.

1524 -- RETURNS TO SPAIN TO LEARN LATIN, THEN STUDIES AT THE UNIVERSITY OF ALCALÁ.

1527 -- IMPRISONED IN SALAMANCA ON SUSPICION OF TEACHING INCORRECTLY. RELEASED AFTER THREE WEEKS, BUT ADMONISHED TO LEARN BEFORE TEACHING MORE.

1528 -- GOES TO PARIS TO STUDY, AND THERE CHANGES HIS NAME TO **IGNATIUS.**

1534 -- AFTER NEARLY SIX YEARS, GRADUATES AS A MASTER OF ARTS. ALONG WITH HIS COMPANIONS, VOWS TO PREACH IN THE HOLY LAND IN A YEAR OR SO.

1537 -- REUNITES WITH HIS COMPANIONS IN VENICE, BUT CONFLICT BETWEEN VENICE AND TURKEY PREVENTS ANY TRAVEL TO JERUSALEM. INSTEAD, THEY TRAVEL TO ROME AND DECIDE TO FORM A RELIGIOUS ORDER.

1540 -- POPE PAUL III APPROVES THE FORMATION OF THE SOCIETY OF JESUS. IGNATIUS IS CHOSEN AS THE FIRST SUPERIOR OF THE SOCIETY.

1548 -- PUBLISHES THE **"SPIRITUAL EXERCISES"** WITH THE APPROVAL OF THE POPE.

1550 -- FOUNDS ROMAN COLLEGE TO TRAIN FUTURE JESUITS.

1556 -- PASSES AWAY AFTER LEADING THE SOCIETY OF JESUS FOR FIFTEEN YEARS.

Have you ever felt alone and mistreated?

SAINT
GERMAINE
OF
PIBRAC

SAINT GERMAINE OF PIBRAC

The Prayer of St. Germaine

St. Germaine, watch over those children who suffer abuse as you did.
Help us to give them the love and protection you only got from God.
Give us the courage to speak out against abuse when we know of it.
Help us to forgive those who abuse the way you forgave,
without sacrificing the lives of the children who need help.
Amen.

GERMAINE COUSIN DIDN'T FOUND A RELIGIOUS ORDER, OR REACH A HIGH CHURCH POST. SHE **DIDN'T** WRITE BOOKS, OR TEACH, OR TRAVEL TO FOREIGN LANDS AS A MISSIONARY. HER ACTIONS WERE **SIMPLE AND KIND,** HER LOVE OF GOD **UNQUESTIONED.**

BORN IN 1579 AND DYING IN 1601, SHE LIVED IN THE LITTLE FRENCH **VILLAGE OF PIBRAC** FOR HER ENTIRE SHORT LIFE. DURING THAT TIME SHE LIVED A LIFE **DEVOTED** TO THE CHURCH AND THE LORD, DESPITE MANY **OBSTACLES.**

GERMAINE IS THE SPECIAL PATRONESS OF VICTIMS OF **ABUSE,** PERSONS WITH **DISABILITIES,** AND **ORPHANS.**

Producer	Editorial	Art	Colors	Letters
Daniel Burton	Kimberly Black	Thomas Gianni	John Rauch	Keith Bahrenburg

The French Village of Pibrac in the Year Of Our Lord 1600, Winter.
Germaine was the daughter of Laurent Cousin, a simple farmer.
STOP!
Her mother, Marie, died soon after the child was born.
COME BACK HERE -- OR YOU'LL BE SORRY!
UN-GRATEFUL GIRL!
Now a widower, Germaine's father had no idea of how to care for a child.
So, being a practical man -- he took the most logical path to a solution.
YOU'LL BE SORRY YOU EVER DISOBEYED ME!

The Outskirts of the Cousin Farm: July 1580.
HELLO, MARIE.
SORRY I HAVEN'T BEEN OUT HERE IN A WHILE, BUT THINGS HAVE BEEN HARD ON THE FARM SINCE YOU PASSED.
THERE'S JUST NEVER ENOUGH TIME.
I CAN'T DO THIS ALONE. I CAN'T RAISE A BABY AND TAKE CARE OF THE SHEEP AND THE FIELDS.
NO ONE MAN COULD. YOU'VE ONLY BEEN GONE A FEW MONTHS, AND I NEED HELP.
SO I WANT YOU TO UNDERSTAND THIS IS NOT JUST FOR ME, BUT FOR GERMAINE AS WELL.
GOD FORGIVE ME, MARIE -- BUT I'VE MET SOMEONE.

Germaine was not an easy baby to care for. She was sickly and suffered from ill health.
Her right hand, being misshapen, prevented her from writing or carrying heavy loads.
As she grew from an infant into a child, her father saw these ailments as weaknesses --
STOP HER!
And as for his new bride, Hortense -- well, she looked upon the child as useless.
FILTHY BEGGAR -- CAN'T EVEN BE BOTHERED TO HELP EXCEPT FOR A COIN OR CRUST OF BREAD!
In the eyes of most, Hortense actively hated the girl.
TUT-TUT. SUCH A SIGHT.
WHICH ONE? THE GIRL OR THE STEP-MOTHER?

The Cousin Farm: August 1587.
SO THIS IS ALL YOU CAN SHOW FOR YOURSELF?
BUT MOTHER, MY HAND KEEPS ME FROM IT.
WHAT?
YOU'VE HAD ALL DAY TO SPIN THAT WOOL, AND YOU'VE BARELY STARTED!
I WILL NOT HEAR YOUR EXCUSES, GERMAINE!

UNDERSTAND THIS, GERMAINE -- I WILL NOT TOLERATE YOUR IDLENESS!
NOW, STOP YOUR SNIVELING AND GET OUT OF MY SIGHT.
AND STAY OUT UNTIL SUPPER!
- SOB -
- SNIFF - WHY DOES SHE HAVE TO BE SO MEAN, LORD?
DOESN'T SHE KNOW SHE NEED NOT FEAR ME OR MY ATTENTION?
I DON'T KNOW WHAT TO DO! I FEEL SO ALONE.

WAIT -- HOW COULD I HAVE BEEN SO SELFISH?
I'M NEVER ALONE -- FOR YOU, LORD, ARE ALWAYS WITH ME.
YOU ARE WATCHING ME EVEN NOW. I KNOW IT.
AND YOU ARE WITH THE REST OF MY FAMILY, TOO. GOD, PLEASE WATCH OVER THEM.
I PRAY FOR MY FATHER IN THE FIELDS, FOR MY NEW BABY BROTHER, AND MY LITTLE SISTER.
AND I PRAY FOR MY STEPMOTHER AND HOPE SHE WILL ACCEPT YOUR LOVE SHE SO DESPERATELY NEEDS.
DEAR LORD, HELP ME TO PLEASE HER, BUT ABOVE ALL, HELP ME TO PLEASE YOU.

Laurent and his new wife went on to have many children.
After the births of what she considered to be her "real" children, Hortense treated Germaine even worse.
All of them were strong and healthy.
OH!
The child was isolated and kept away from her brothers and sisters.
This was probably a blessing for Germaine, after all, because Hortense had turned her children against the young girl.

The Cousin Farm: May 1594.
HURRY, SHE'S COMING!
GOT THEM!
– GIGGLE –
– HEE HEE –
GERMAINE, COME AND EAT WITH US. MOTHER MADE YOUR FAVORITE.
– GAKL –
TASTY, ISN'T IT?

GERMAINE!
WHAT HAS HAPPENED? CAN'T WE HAVE ANY PEACE IN THIS HOUSE?
I'LL TAKE CARE OF IT, LAURENT. SIT AND EAT.
GERMAINE? I KNOW YOU'RE HIDING.
WELL, IF YOU WON'T COME OUT --
AND YOU LIKE THIS SMELLY OLD BARN SO MUCH --
YOU CAN LIVE IN HERE FROM NOW ON.
PRAYING AGAIN, I SEE? WELL, PRAYING ISN'T GOING TO CHANGE ANYTHING.
THAT'S WHERE YOU'RE WRONG, MOTHER.
PRAYER IS POWERFUL.

With such treatment at home, Germaine became quiet and rarely spoke.
NOW, I'VE GOT YOU!
She saved her voice for communicating with God.
Because she knew the Lord was always listening and would watch out for her.
HOLD YOUR HAND, HORTENSE.
As on this particular day, when He sent me into the street.
I had seen too much. Such cruelty could no longer be allowed to go unchecked.
HASN'T THIS CHILD SUFFERED ENOUGH?

FATHER REMY! I MIGHT HAVE KNOWN YOU'D TRY AND INTERFERE.
WELL, THIS TIME, YOU'LL SEE WHAT I HAVE TO DEAL WITH! GO AHEAD, YOU LITTLE THIEF! SHOW HIM WHAT YOU'RE HIDING IN YOUR APRON!
GERMAINE, IS THIS TRUE? DID YOU STEAL SOMETHING FROM YOUR MOTHER?
SHE IS NOT MY MOTHER, AND I TOOK NOTHING.
LIAR!
HORTENSE, PLEASE. LET THE GIRL SPEAK.

I AM **NO THIEF**. WHAT I TOOK IS **MINE** TO DO WITH AS **I WISH**.
AND **WHAT** DID YOU **TAKE**, GERMAINE?
SHOW HIM! SHOW HIM **THE FOOD** YOU STOLE FROM YOUR **OWN FAMILY** --
TO **FEED** THE FILTHY BEGGARS THAT **SLEEP** IN THE GUTTERS OF **OUR VILLAGE!**
NO CHILD **OF MINE** WOULD DO SUCH **THINGS** -- BUT YOU'RE **NOT MY CHILD**, ARE YOU?
JUST AN **UGLY CRIPPLE** WITH A DISEASED **MIND!** WHAT DO YOU HAVE **TO SAY** FOR YOURSELF?
I SAY -- THAT I **FORGIVE YOU**.
A hush fell over the crowd with those simple words.

YOU DARE! YOU SAY YOU FORGIVE ME? I'VE HAD ENOUGH OF THIS, GERMAINE!
RETURN THAT BREAD THIS INSTANT!
It was then we witnessed the miracle.
For held within Germaine's apron were not a few crusts of bread, but flowers.
Fresh wildflowers. The wildflowers of summer.
Flowers unseen in our village for months, yet appearing to have been picked but mere moments ago.
All of us, even cruel Hortense, drank in the sight of those flowers.

After that day, no one in the village of Pibrac ever looked at Germaine again with pity or contempt.
No one whispered about her face, or pointed at her withered hand. Neither her tattered clothing nor lack of shoes was laughed at.
Instead, the good heart within the misshapen body was seen fully at last, and she was loved.
After that day, she was venerated and adored ... even by her parents.
Laurent Cousin stopped grieving for a wife lost, and learned to love the child from their union.

The Outlying Regions of the Cousin Farm: May 1601.
I became a scribe, keeping an account of Germaine's life. She confided some of the details to me, while others were from my own observation.
The cold of that miracle winter gave way to a new year, and it was a typical spring day for Germaine in the fields.
As always, her duties were to tend the sheep.
But no longer was she asked to try and spin their wool into cloth.
This never upset the girl, even though the chore kept her far away from people.
SUCH A BEAUTIFUL DAY, ISN'T IT, LITTLE ONE?
For fear Germaine's skin disease was contagious, Hortense sent her into the fields.
A GLORIOUS MORNING TO BE OUTSIDE, SURROUNDED BY THE GLORIES OF GOD.
BONG! BONG! BONG!
OH! TIME FOR MASS!
Now, she had been asked back into the warmth of her home, but the girl refused.
She told her parents the outdoors and the barn were her homes now.

I knew the only thing that separated Germaine from her guardianship in the pasture was the ringing of the church bell to summon worshippers to Mass.
Unlike other shepherdesses in the village, she worried not for her flock.
She knew heavenly eyes would watch over the helpless sheep while she attended services.
Germaine told me when she returned from the church, all was as she left it.
Not a single sheep was ever missing.
Not one.

GERMAINE -- DOES ALL OF THE ATTENTION YOU NOW RECEIVE EVER MAKE YOU FEEL UNCOMFORT-ABLE?
FATHER REMY, PEOPLE HAVE ALWAYS STARED AT ME.
I COULD HIDE MY CROOKED HAND, BUT MY FACE HELD THEIR ATTENTION NO MATTER WHERE I WENT.
HELPING TO DO THE WORK OF THE LORD IS MY GREATEST DESIRE AND I AM HONORED THAT HE WOULD USE ME.
HE IS MY GUARDIAN, MY PARENT, AND MY SHEPHERD.

So it was, the very next day, Germaine did not appear to take her sheep out to pasture.
Laurent Cousin, even though forgiven by his daughter, was still weighed down with guilt over how he had treated her over the years.
He went in search of her and found that the young woman had passed and was lying peacefully in the barn.
Her life of suffering was over, and yet her absence has created a void that each of us will have to fill through the presence of God.
As was fitting, we buried Germaine here, within the church of Pibrac. Her resting place was directly across from the pulpit.
On the day of her burial, the entire village wept.

A Saint's Journey

WE KNOW LITTLE FOR CERTAIN ABOUT THE CHRONOLOGY OF GERMAINE COUSIN'S LIFE, BUT WE DO KNOW THAT IN **1579**, SHE WAS BORN IN **PIBRAC**, A SMALL VILLAGE IN THE **OCCITAN REGION** OF **SOUTHERN FRANCE**, TO **LAURENT COUSIN** AND **MARIE LAROCHE**.

GERMAINE LIVED DURING A TUMULTUOUS TIME. FOR DECADES, THE RELIGIOUS CONFLICTS BETWEEN **CATHOLICS** AND **HUGUENOTS** HAD RAVAGED FRANCE. VIOLENCE, FAMINE, AND DISEASE KILLED THREE MILLION PEOPLE IN THIRTY-SIX YEARS AND LEFT SURVIVORS DESTITUTE.

GERMAINE'S FAMILY DID NOT ESCAPE THESE TRAGEDIES. ONCE THE OWNER OF A **PROSPEROUS** FARM, LAURENT COUSIN WAS LIVING IN POVERTY WHEN GERMAINE WAS BORN. **MARIE** DIED NOT LONG AFTER GIVING BIRTH. UNABLE TO CARE FOR HIS DAUGHTER ALONE, LAURENT MARRIED A WOMAN NAMED **HORTENSE**.

AS A CHILD, GERMAINE CONTRACTED A KIND OF TUBERCULOSIS KNOWN AS **SCROFULA**, WHICH DISFIGURED HER **FACE** AND **NECK**. HER RIGHT HAND WAS MISSHAPEN. EVEN WITH THESE PHYSICAL DEFECTS, GERMAINE POSSESSED A RADIANT **INNER** BEAUTY.

THOSE WHO KNEW AND LOVED HER SAID SHE WAS "SO GREATLY **ENLIGHTENED** BY THE GIFTS OF DIVINE WISDOM AND UNDERSTANDING, AND SO REMARKABLE FOR HER TRANSCENDENT VIRTUES, THAT SHE SHONE LIKE A **STAR**," ACCORDING TO BUTLER'S "LIVES OF THE SAINTS."

THOSE WHO DID NOT RECOGNIZE GERMAINE'S HOLINESS, HOWEVER, MISTREATED HER TERRIBLY. STILL, GERMAINE PRAYED EVERY DAY FOR HER NEGLIGENT FATHER, HER ABUSIVE STEPMOTHER, AND HER CRUEL STEPSIBLINGS.

WHEN SHE BECAME A **SHEPHERDESS** AT THE YOUNG AGE OF **NINE**, GERMAINE SPENT HER TIME IN THE FIELDS CONTEMPLATING GOD'S GREAT LOVE FOR HER AND FOR THE POOR, FOR WHOM SHE HAD GREAT COMPASSION. OFTEN, GERMAINE BROUGHT FOOD TO THE MANY **BEGGARS** IN HER VILLAGE. ONE WINTER, SHE WAS CAUGHT TAKING A LOAF OF BREAD, BUT WHEN SHE OPENED HER APRON, WILDFLOWERS CAME **TUMBLING OUT!** EVERYONE, EVEN CRUEL HORTENSE, KNEW THEN THAT THE YOUNG WOMAN WAS A GREAT SAINT.

GERMAINE'S LONGING, THOUGH, WAS NOT FOR WORLDLY RENOWN, BUT FOR THE **LOVING** EMBRACE OF HER HEAVENLY FATHER.

ONE SPRING MORNING IN **1601**, WHEN GERMAINE WAS **TWENTY-TWO**, HER WISH CAME TRUE. TRAVELERS NEAR PIBRAC SAW HER SOUL ASCENDING TO HEAVEN, SHROUDED IN **LIGHT** AND **ESCORTED BY ANGELS**.

CANONIZED ON **JUNE 29, 1867**, BY POPE PIUS IX, GERMAINE IS THE PATRONESS OF **ABUSE VICTIMS**.

Who has shown you mercy?

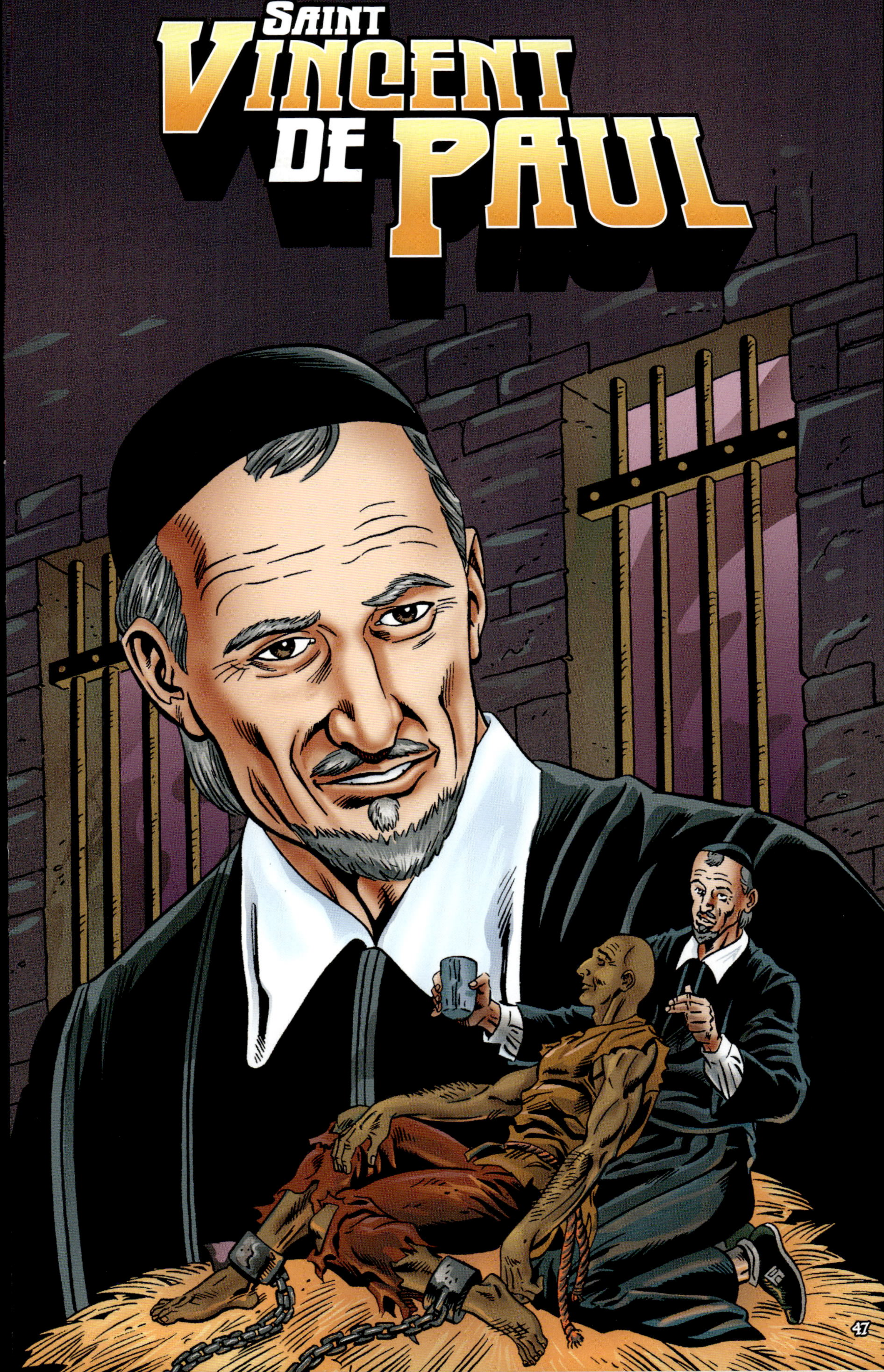
SAINT
VINCENT
DE PAUL

SAINT VINCENT DE PAUL

"Extend mercy toward others, so that there can be no one in need whom you meet without helping. For what hope is there for us if God should withdraw His mercy from us?"

--From the Writings of St. Vincent de Paul

CHARITY.

IT WAS ***MANY YEARS*** INTO HIS STUDIES WHEN VINCENT DE PAUL DISCOVERED THAT HIS HEART MUST BE ***GIVING*** TO DO THE LORD'S WORK.

AND FOR ANY OF US TO EXPERIENCE TRULY THE ***LIGHT*** AND ***LOVE*** OF GOD, WE ALSO MUST HELP TO ***STOP THE SUFFERING*** OF OUR FELLOW MAN.

IF A BEGGAR IS HUNGRY,
GIVE HIM FOOD TO EAT.

IF A CHILD IS COLD,
GIVE HIM A COAT.

IF AN ELDER IS SICK,
GIVE HIM MEDICINE.

BASIC HUMAN KINDNESS. IN SUCH ACTIONS WE FIND THE ***TRUE*** MEANING OF THE WORDS OF JESUS CHRIST.

VINCENT DE PAUL UNDERSTOOD THIS SIMPLE RULE OF LIFE, AND SHARED IT WITH EVERYONE HE MET.

Producer: *Daniel Burton* Editorial: *Kimberly Black*
Story: *Terry Collins* Pencils: *Rod Whigham*
Inker: *Al Milgrom* Letters: *Keith Bahrenburg*
Colors and Design: *Daniel Burton*

January 19, 1617. The Picardy region of France.
The Folleville Chateau of Countess de Gondi, Lady of the House of Philip de Gondi, Count of Joigny.
MONSIEUR VINCENT, COME QUICKLY!
THERE'S BEEN AN ACCIDENT -- YOU ARE NEEDED! PLEASE HURRY!
OF COURSE --
A MOMENT, WHILE I GATHER MY THINGS.
NOW -- WHAT HAS HAPPENED, CHILD?
A PEASANT WAS WORKING PAST SUNDOWN. IN THE DARKNESS, HE FELL UNDER THE WHEELS OF HIS WAGON.

HAS THE COUNTESS BEEN NOTIFIED?
YES, FATHER. I WAS SENT TO FETCH YOU BY MADAME DE GONDI HERSELF.
I SEE.
GOOD EVENING, MADAME.
GOOD EVENING, VINCENT.
I CAN THINK OF FEW NOBLES WHO WOULD TAKE SUCH AN INTEREST IN MÉTAYERS.*
AS YOU HAVE TOLD ME MANY TIMES, COMPASSION HAS NO BEARING ON STATUS OR CLASS.
*MÉTAYERS: FARMERS WHO WERE PROVIDED WITH SUPPLIES AND LAND BY WEALTHY NOBLES AND LANDOWNERS, IN RETURN FOR HALF OF THE CROP AT HARVEST TIME.

YOUR HEART IS KIND, COUNTESS.
I AM HUMBLED YOU WOULD ACCOMPANY ME ON THIS GRIM TASK.
WHEN YOU WERE RECOMMENDED TO MY FAMILY AS A TEACHER, I MERELY SAW AN EDUCATED MAN TO TUTOR MY CHILDREN.
BUT YOUR SPIRITUAL GUIDANCE HAS BEEN A REVELATION FOR ME.
TAKE YOUR GENEROSITY OF OFFERING COUNSEL TO A DYING PEASANT ON MY ESTATE. SUCH DEEDS INSPIRE ME, VINCENT, AND MAKE ME WANT TO HELP OTHERS.
GOD PLACES US WHERE WE CAN BE OF THE BEST USE.
MY HUSBAND AND I WEIGH YOUR IDEAS, AND YOUR WORDS, WITH THE UTMOST CARE.
I AM PRIVILEGED TO BE SUCH A POSITIVE INFLUENCE, MADAME.

THANK YOU FOR COMING, MONSIEUR.
MY HUSBAND, GILLES -- HE HAS STRUGGLED TO HOLD ON TO GIVE HIS FINAL CONFESSION.
I AM HAPPY TO BE OF SERVICE, AND DO NOT WORRY, GOOD WOMAN.
GILLES SHALL ENTER THE GATES OF HEAVEN WITH A CLEAN HEART.
I AM DYING, FATHER.
REST EASY, MY SON. GOD IS WITH YOU.
THROUGH THIS HOLY ANOINTING MAY THE LORD IN HIS LOVE AND MERCY HELP YOU WITH THE GRACE OF THE HOLY SPIRIT.
MAY THE LORD WHO FREES YOU FROM SIN SAVE YOU AND RAISE YOU UP --
"AND LET THEM PRAY OVER HIM, ANOINTING HIM WITH OIL IN THE NAME OF THE LORD."*
*JAMES 5:14

FATHER -- I WISH TO MAKE A FINAL CONFESSION, BUT I FEAR I DO NOT KNOW HOW.
HAVE YOU TRIED YOUR BEST TO LIVE FOR THE LORD EVERY DAY?
SADLY, MONSIEUR, I HAVE NOT. AND NOW ON MY DEATHBED, I FEAR I HAVE WASTED MY LIFE.
NO LIFE LIVED IS WASTED. LIFE IS A GIFT OF OUR LORD AND SAVIOR, JESUS CHRIST.
HAVE YOU NOW, REALIZING YOUR MISTAKE, EXAMINED YOUR CONSCIENCE, MY SON?
MY CONSCIENCE? NO, NO I HAVE NOT.
THEN NOW IS THE TIME TO DO SO. GOD IS ALWAYS THERE; WE HAVE ONLY TO CALL ON HIM.
ALL YOU NEED TO DO IS OPEN YOUR HEART, AND SPEAK WHAT IS WITHIN. THE TRUTH WILL SET YOU FREE.
NOW, MAKE YOUR GENERAL CONFESSION.
I WILL BE YOUR GUIDE -- GOD WILL GIVE YOU COMFORT AND PEACE.

YOU WERE DESTINED TO BE AT THAT PEASANT'S SIDE TO ATTEND HIM LAST NIGHT, MONSIEUR VINCENT.
GILLES, MY LADY. HIS NAME WAS GILLES.
TO THINK, ALL THOSE YEARS HE HAD ATTENDED MASS AND HIS HEART HAD NOT BEEN FULLY GIVEN OVER TO CHRIST. HOW MANY OTHER CHRISTIANS ARE LIVING IN THE SAME FALSEHOOD?
WHEN I SAT BY HIS SIDE, GILLES WAS LOST. HE HADN'T TRULY EXPERIENCED ANY OF GOD'S GRACE.
INDEED, THAT IS UNFORTU- NATE.
HE WAS REMORSEFUL TO BE SURE, BUT KNEW NOTHING OF HIS FAITH OR CONVICTION.
HE HAD BEEN CARRYING HEAVY BURDENS ALL HIS LIFE, WHICH HAD NEVER BEEN CONFESSED -- HE NEEDED ONLY TO CONFESS FOR THE LORD TO HEAR HIS PRAYER AND GRANT HIM PARDON.

Last night, after returning to the chateau, I prayed for hours.
I realized Gilles was but one of many caught in this terrible spiritual state.
And then, a passage from the New Testament came to me... Jesus was sent to preach the gospel to the poor, to bind up the brokenhearted, to proclaim freedom to the captives!
That is the answer to the question I have carried within me all these years! I have been a loyal servant of the Lord, but a man without direction.
GOD HAS SHOWN ME THE PATH I SHOULD FOLLOW. I MUST REACH OUT TO THE NEEDY AND PRESENT THE GOSPEL IN A WAY THEY CAN TRULY UNDERSTAND.
I HOPE YOU DO NOT PLAN TO LEAVE MY EMPLOY, MONSIEUR.
ON THE CONTRARY, FOR THERE IS MUCH WORK TO BE DONE RIGHT HERE.
THE NEED FOR RELIGIOUS INSTRUCTION AMONG THE PEASANTS OF YOUR ESTATES MUST BE MET.
IF GUIDANCE IS NEEDED TO SHOW THEM THE WAY, YOU HAVE MY FULL SUPPORT.

January 25, 1617. The Church of Folleville.
VINCENT, THERE IS A SMALL CHURCH IN THE VILLAGE --
YES, MADAME. I KNOW OF IT.
PERHAPS YOU SHOULD BEGIN PREACHING YOUR MESSAGE OF GUIDANCE THERE.
I WILL SEE TO IT THAT EVERYONE KNOWS THE IMPORTANCE OF WHAT YOU PLAN TO SAY, AND THAT THEY SHOULD ATTEND YOUR SUNDAY SERVICE.
LORD, ASSIST ME IN PRESENTING YOUR DIVINE WISDOM TO THE FLOCK GATHERED WITHIN YOUR HOUSE ON THIS BEAUTIFUL MORNING.

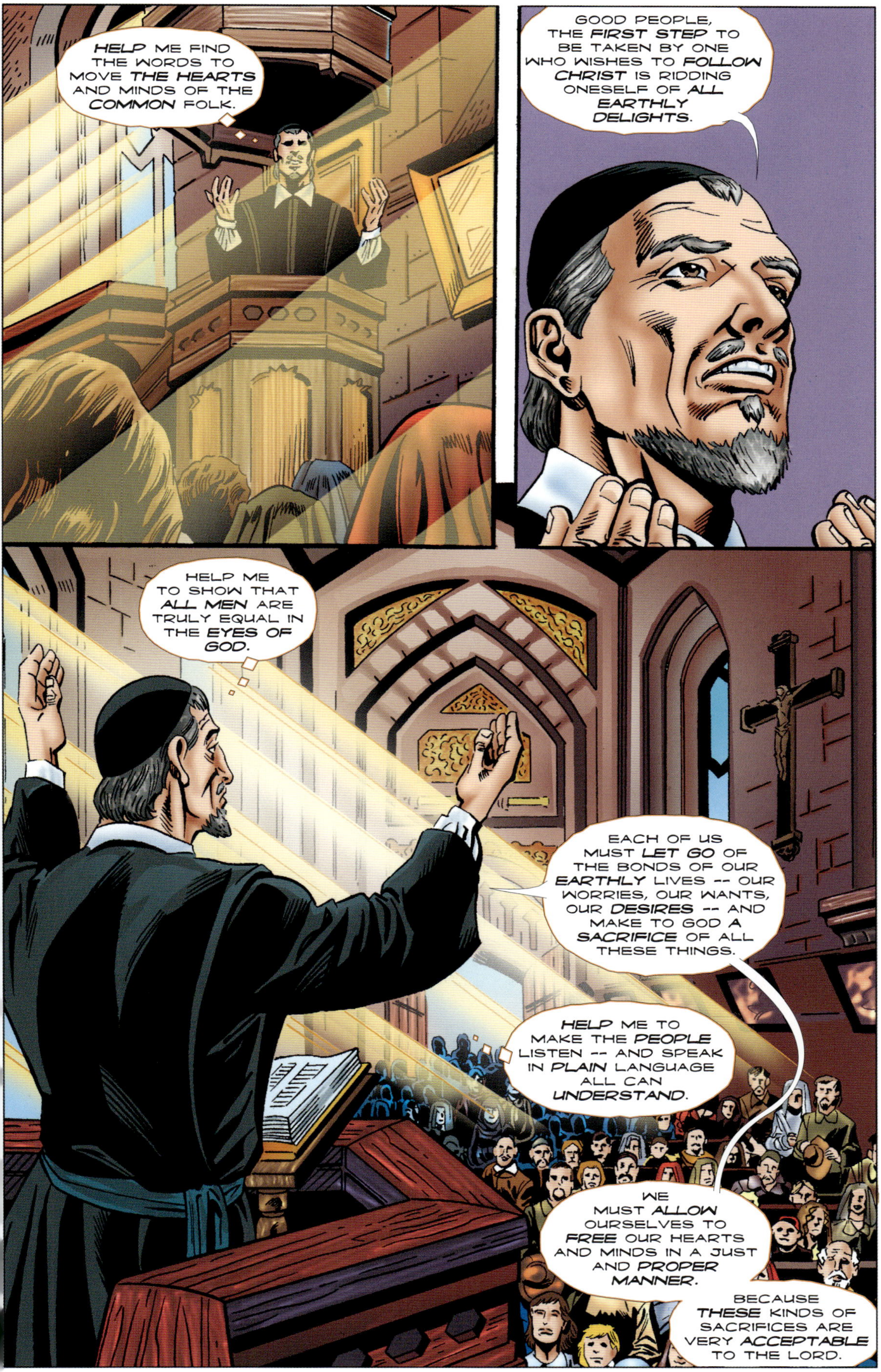
HELP ME FIND THE WORDS TO MOVE THE HEARTS AND MINDS OF THE COMMON FOLK.
GOOD PEOPLE, THE FIRST STEP TO BE TAKEN BY ONE WHO WISHES TO FOLLOW CHRIST IS RIDDING ONESELF OF ALL EARTHLY DELIGHTS.
HELP ME TO SHOW THAT ALL MEN ARE TRULY EQUAL IN THE EYES OF GOD.
EACH OF US MUST LET GO OF THE BONDS OF OUR EARTHLY LIVES -- OUR WORRIES, OUR WANTS, OUR DESIRES -- AND MAKE TO GOD A SACRIFICE OF ALL THESE THINGS.
HELP ME TO MAKE THE PEOPLE LISTEN -- AND SPEAK IN PLAIN LANGUAGE ALL CAN UNDERSTAND.
WE MUST ALLOW OURSELVES TO FREE OUR HEARTS AND MINDS IN A JUST AND PROPER MANNER.
BECAUSE THESE KINDS OF SACRIFICES ARE VERY ACCEPTABLE TO THE LORD.

PEOPLE OF FRANCE, I ASK OF YOU TO TAKE TO HEART THE NECESSITY OF REPENTANCE.
COME FORWARD THIS DAY, AND CONFESS YOUR SINS.
I WILL BE THE FIRST TO CONFESS TODAY, FATHER VINCENT.
NOW I ASK, WHO WILL FOLLOW ME?
THE CHURCH IS FOR ALL GOD'S CHILDREN, RICH AND POOR, PEASANTS AND NOBLES, THE SOPHISTICATED AND THE SIMPLE.
ALL ARE WELCOME. GOD IS WAITING.

April 17, 1625. The College des Bons-Enfants, Paris.
The first official meeting of the Congregation of the Mission.
WE ARE GLAD YOU HAVE CALLED US, VINCENT. TO BE A PART OF ORGANIZING THIS GRAND GROUP IS TRULY TO BE A PART OF HISTORY.
THE ARCHBISHOP OF PARIS HAS GIVEN THE AUTHORIZATION TO BRING ABOUT THE SALVATION OF THE POOR COUNTRY PEOPLE.
EIGHT YEARS AFTER YOU GATHERED THE CROWDS IN FOLLEVILLE TO MAKE THEIR GENERAL CONFESSIONS, YOUR LEGEND CONTINUES TO GROW.
WE ARE HONORED TO SERVE YOU.
I AM BUT A HUMBLE SERVANT OF THE LORD.
THE LEGEND IS HOW THE PEOPLE EMBRACED THE WORD OF JESUS CHRIST.
AND WE SERVE NO MAN, ONLY GOD.
OF COURSE, I MEANT NO DISRESPECT.

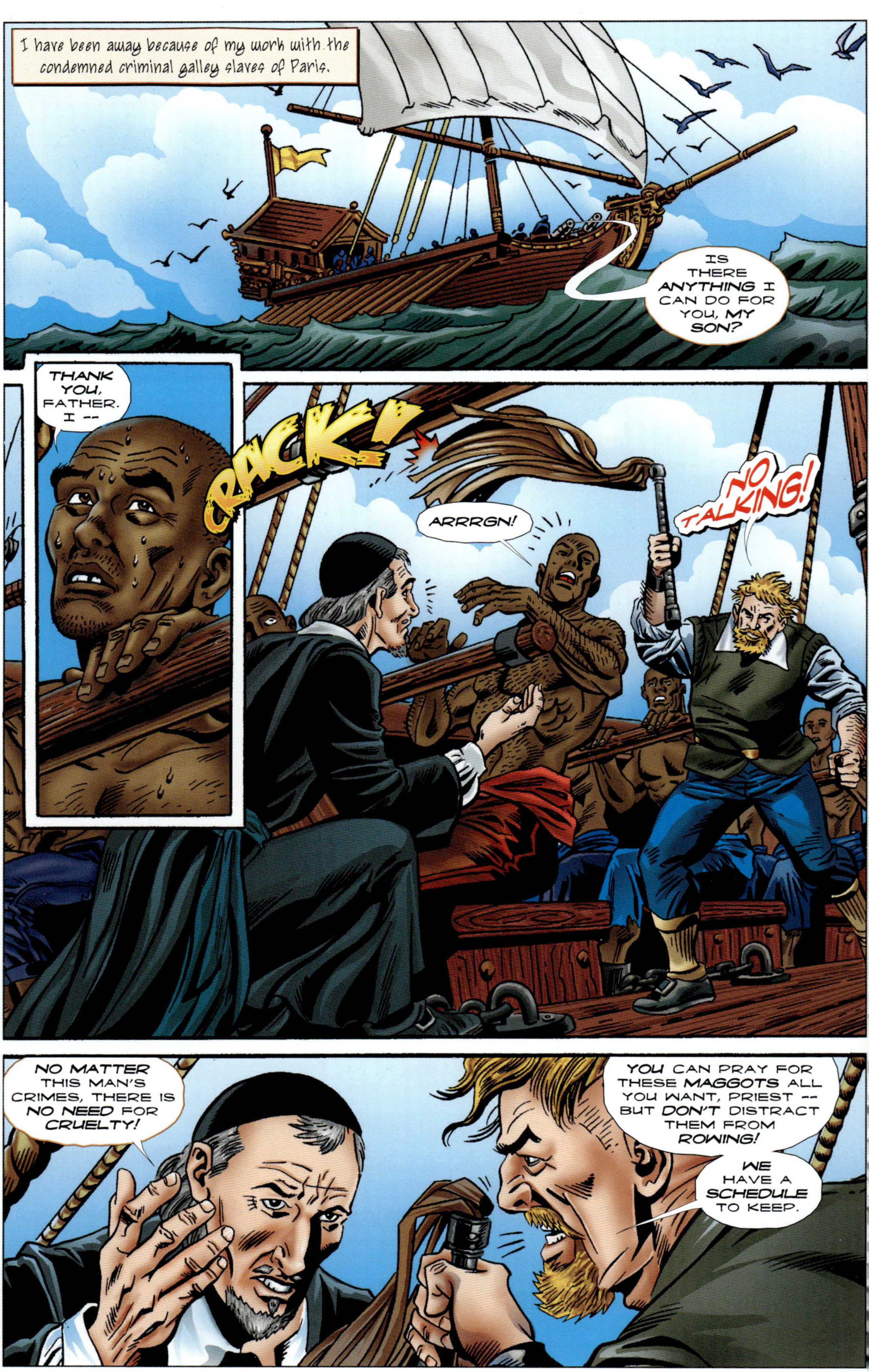

I have been away because of my work with the condemned criminal galley slaves of Paris.
IS THERE ANYTHING I CAN DO FOR YOU, MY SON?
THANK YOU, FATHER. I --
CRACK!
ARRRGN!
NO TALKING!
NO MATTER THIS MAN'S CRIMES, THERE IS NO NEED FOR CRUELTY!
YOU CAN PRAY FOR THESE MAGGOTS ALL YOU WANT, PRIEST -- BUT DON'T DISTRACT THEM FROM ROWING!
WE HAVE A SCHEDULE TO KEEP.

UNCHAIN THIS MAN, AND I SHALL TAKE HIS PLACE.
I AM UNBOWED, AND CAN SURELY ROW FASTER THAN HE.
JUST REST, MY SON. REST UNTIL WE REACH OUR DESTINATION.
BLESS YOU, MONSIEUR VINCENT.
WHY ARE YOU DOING THIS?
ALL OF YOU ARE MY BROTHERS, AND WE ARE ALL THE CHILDREN OF THE KINGDOM OF HEAVEN.
YOU'LL NEVER MAKE IT, MONSIEUR. ALREADY YOUR HANDS HAVE BEGUN TO BLEED.
MY SON, IF WE DON'T EXTEND MERCY TOWARD OTHERS, WHAT HOPE IS THERE FOR US IF GOD SHOULD WITHDRAW HIS MERCY FROM US?

After rowing well into the night, we found our way back to the Paris docks.
Before the galley slaves were led into their dank cells, I blessed each of them, ignoring the ache in my shoulders, and the pain of my torn hands.
Their salvation was worth any discomfort I might feel, but still I wondered ... what else could I offer to these men?
Then, the Lord revealed to me what was needed. This group of slaves was but a mere sampling.
WAIT!
A WASTE OF YOUR TIME, MONSIEUR, FOR YOU TO ENTER THIS HOUSE OF THE UNWANTED.
To be truly effective, I needed to carry the word of God into the very prisons themselves.
GOD ISN'T TO BE FOUND DOWN HERE.
HE IS NOW.

Day after day, I lived among the prisoners. At times, even my own heart grew heavy from the smell and the darkness and the despair.
IS IT TRUE, FATHER? IS THIS HELL?
NO, MY SON -- PRISON IS BUT A SECOND CHANCE.
YOU CAN RECANT YOUR SINS, RECEIVE ABSOLUTION -- LIFE DOES NOT END ON THIS EARTHLY PLANE.
IT IS NOT TOO LATE TO RECEIVE THE GRACE OF GOD.
I KNEW YOU WERE AN ANGEL WHEN YOU SAVED ME THAT DAY ON THE SHIP, FATHER.
I HAVE THREE MORE YEARS TO SPEND IN THE GALLEYS -- EVEN IF I SURVIVE, I WILL BE A BROKEN MAN.
IF YOU SAY GOD CARES, THEN I WILL GLADLY ACCEPT HIS BLESSING.
GOD CARES FOR ALL OF US.
AND KNOW THIS -- WHEN YOU ARE RELEASED, I WILL BE WAITING FOR YOU.
The conditions in which those slaves toiled were unimaginable, but I did what I could to comfort them.

YOUR SACRIFICES ARE INCREDIBLE!
WE SHALL ALL MAKE SUCH SACRIFICES BEFORE OUR WORK IS DONE.
EVEN THOUGH THEIR IMPRISONED BODIES ARE CONFINED, THEIR SOULS REMAIN FREE.
WITH THEIR CONFESSIONS, THE MEN KNOW THEY ARE DESTINED FOR HEAVEN.
SUCH, AS ALWAYS, IS THE CLOSE LINK BETWEEN SAVING THE LOST, AND SERVING THE POOR.
WHAT WE DO IN THE CONTRACT BROUGHT FORTH ON THIS DAY IS TO SERVE CHRIST IN THE PERSON OF THE UNFORTUNATE.
CHRIST WAS SENT HERE BY THE FATHER TO EVANGELIZE THE NEEDY, AND WE IN TURN MUST KEEP THIS MISSION CENTRAL TO OUR MINISTRY.
WE WILL DEDICATE OURSELVES TO THE SALVATION OF THE POOR.
NOW JOIN ME IN TAKING THE VOWS OF POVERTY, CHASTITY, OBEDIENCE, AND STABILITY, AS WE DEVOTE OURSELVES TO THE PEOPLE IN THE SMALLER TOWNS AND VILLAGES.
THE ENDOWMENT TO FOUND OUR WORK FROM THE COUNTESS DE GONDI HAS GIVEN US OUR BEGINNINGS -- NOW WE MUST GO FORTH AND SPREAD GOD'S WORD.
VINCENT, I DO NOT KNOW IF YOU HAVE HEARD, BUT THE COUNTESS IS ILL.
THE COUNTESS? I MUST LEAVE AT ONCE!
I SHALL ATTEND YOU.

The Folleville Chateau of Countess de Gondi.
WHY DIDN'T YOU SEND FOR ME? AS YOUR SPIRITUAL DIRECTOR, I SHOULD HAVE BEEN TOLD.
I DIDN'T WANT TO INTERRUPT YOUR MINISTRY, MONSIEUR VINCENT.
BESIDES, IF YOU WERE MEANT TO BE HERE, I KNEW GOD WOULD SEND YOU.
NOW, WILL YOU HEAR MY FINAL CONFESSION, MONSIEUR VINCENT?
YES COUNTESS, REST ASSURED, YOU HAVE ALWAYS BEEN MOST GENEROUS AND KIND -- ALWAYS HONEST AND PENITENT.
SIT WITH ME, HUMBLE VINCENT -- JUST FOR A SHORT WHILE. I DO NOT THINK I WILL BE A PART OF THIS WORLD MUCH LONGER.

June 1625. The de Gondi family cemetery.
Even in death, you inspire me, Countess. I will seek out other benefactors ... the wealthy women of Paris are a resource to collect funds to help the sick.
The Congregation of the Mission shall widen our goals to build hospitals, for it is our duty to service the poor as quickly, and as completely, as possible.
As always, the Lord's work is truly never done.
PARDON ME, VINCENT -- BUT IT IS URGENT NEWS: YOU ARE NEEDED IN TOWN IMMEDIATELY!
IF SUMMONED, I AM THERE.

A Saint's Journey

APRIL 24, 1581 / Vincent de Paul is born in the village of Pouy, near Dax, in Gascony, France. He is the third of six children (four sons, two daughters).

C. 1595–1597 / A young Vincent begins his studies for the priesthood.

1600 / Vincent is ordained a priest by the Bishop of Périgueux, François de Bourdeilles, at the young age of nineteen.

1604 / Vincent receives his bachelor of theology from the University of Toulouse.

1613 / The Count and Countess of Joigny, of the de Gondi family, hire Vincent as tutor to their children, and chaplain of the de Gondi estates.

1617 / At the urging of the countess, Vincent preaches his famed sermon on general confession at the Church of Folleville.

1619 / Concerned with the plight of the galley slaves of France, Vincent is appointed as their chaplain.

1622 / Vincent founds a mission for the galley slaves at Bordeaux.

1625 / In April, Vincent oversees the first official meeting of the Congregation of the Mission at the Collége des Bons-Enfants in Paris. Two months later, the Countess de Gondi, one of Vincent's lifelong supporters, dies.

1633 / Vincent co-founds the Daughters of Charity with Louise de Marillac to serve the sick and the poor.

1660 / Vincent dies peacefully in Paris at nearly eighty years old.

1737 / Vincent is canonized by Pope Clement XII.

Where is your place of solitude?

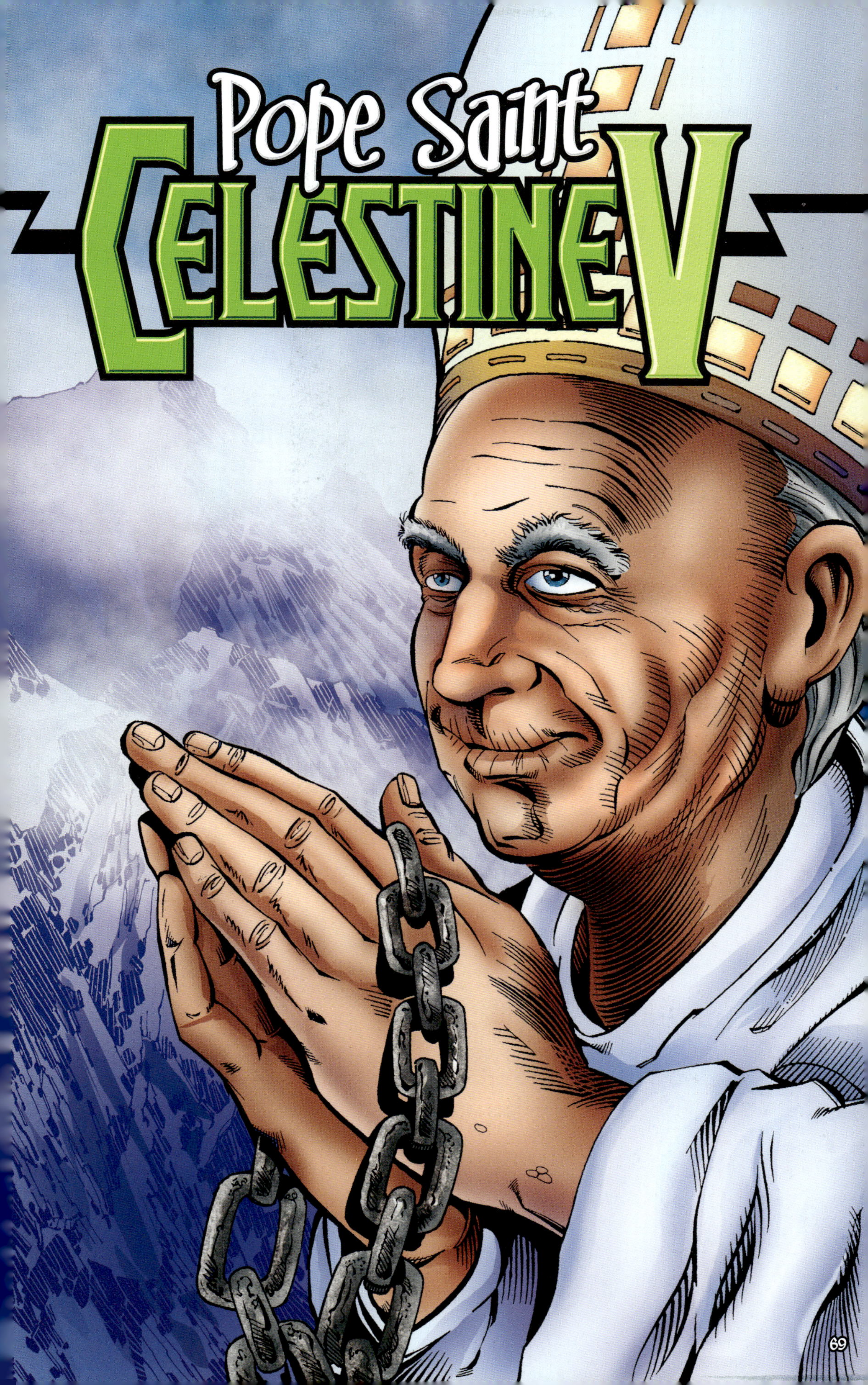
Pope Saint
CELESTINE V

Pope Saint Celestine V

Pope St. Celestine V was the founder of the Order of the Benedictine Celestines and a lover of solitude. Devoted to pious, sacrificial living, Pope Celestine V, previously known as Pietro di Murrone, spent much of his life pursuing silence, reflection, and seclusion. The role of pope never seemed to sit well with Celestine V, who was a unique and troubled soul. A hermit at heart, Pope Celestine V served as pope for only a short amount of time until he resigned amid great scandal and protest.

Pope Celestine V is remembered mostly for his great faith and devotion to a strict, disciplined life of piety. He wore chains around his neck and often fasted for days on end in order to commune more closely with the Holy Spirit and to remind himself to think on things above. Unanimously elected pope in 1294 at age seventy-nine, Celestine felt he could not ignore God's calling and sacrificed his life of solitude for that of public service. His cardinals, split by political affiliations, offered him little help, and in return he sought little aid while serving five short months as pope. A simple man of the Lord, Celestine was not made for politics and found himself cruelly used by King Charles of Naples and other scheming individuals.

After the unprecedented resignation of his papacy, St. Celestine was segregated by Pope Boniface VIII to the tower in the castle of Fumone, where he lived out the rest of his days in seclusion. One wonders if these last months brought him the privacy he desired but had never truly achieved in his eighty-one years on this earth.

producer Daniel Burton
story Jen Murvin Edwards
inks Claude St. Aubin
letters Keith Bahrenburg
editor Kimberly Black
pencils Lou Manna
colors Mark McNabb
design Jeff Dawidowski

MAY 1296. CASTLE OF FUMONE. LAZIO, ITALY.
WHO WOULD'VE THOUGHT IT WOULD END LIKE THIS?
I REMEMBER ...

1260. WILDS OF MT. MURRONE, ITALY.
THERE HE IS -- PIETRO DI MURRONE! I CAN'T BELIEVE WE ACTUALLY FOUND HIM; THE OTHER BROTHERS HAVE BEEN SEARCHING FOR DAYS!
JUST LOOK AT HIM --
HE IS THE IMAGE OF THE BAPTIST! NEVER HAVE I SEEN A MAN SO HOLY.
WHY DOES HE WANT TO STAY HERE IN THE WOODS?
SO MANY OF US WANT HIM TO COME DOWN, START AN ORDER ---
BUT HE JUST KEEPS CLIMBING!
HE IS THE MOST PRIVATE AND SOLITARY OF MEN.
ALTHOUGH HE HAS ALMOST THREE HUNDRED FOLLOWERS, HE WISHES TO KEEP TO HIMSELF!
TO MAINTAIN A CONSTANT COMMUNION WITH THE LORD, A LIFE OF PIETY, SACRIFICE!
I AM SURE THAT IF WE TOO FOLLOW THE SAME RULE OF LIFE AS THIS MAN, TRULY, BROTHER, WE WILL BE CLOSER WITH THE LORD.
NOW THAT WE KNOW WHERE HE IS, LET'S GET THE OTHERS! MAYBE TOGETHER WE CAN PERSUADE HIM.

1284. ORDER OF THE BENEDICTINE CELESTINES.
THIRTY YEARS! I AM HONORED, LORD, THAT YOU WOULD WORK THROUGH ME.
BUT EVEN AFTER ALL THIS TIME, I STILL LONG TO BE ALONE. ALONE WITH YOU!
THE FREEDOM ...
SUPERVISION OF MEN IS LOST ON ME ... AND I AM ALMOST SEVENTY YEARS OLD. THIS BROTHER WILL DO A FINE JOB TAKING OVER. I WILL SPEND THE REMAINDER OF MY DAYS WHERE I LONG TO BE ...
OUT THERE.
BUT THERE IS NO WAY HE COULD HAVE KNOWN ...

TEN YEARS LATER. NAPLES.
TWO YEARS AND THE CONCLAVE HAS NOT ELECTED A POPE! THOSE CARDINALS -- THEY HAVE DEBATED TOO LONG! IT'S GETTING IN MY WAY!
KING CHARLES, THE CONCLAVE IS SPLIT! THE TWO FACTIONS DIVIDE THE CARDINALS, AND NEITHER HAS THE MAJORITY. THEY VOTE AND VOTE, BUT IT JUST GOES AROUND IN CIRCLES.
IF THIS CYCLE KEEPS HAPPENING, WE MAY NEVER GET A POPE!
BUT WHAT SHOULD I DO? MY HANDS ARE TIED!
WITHOUT A POPE, THE GOVERNMENT HAS NO SPIRITUAL GUIDANCE. NOT TO MENTION, WITHOUT PAPAL AUTHORITY I CAN'T EXPAND THE NATION!
YOU CAN'T APPEAR TO HAVE LOST CONTROL. YOU MUST BE PATIENT, YOUR MAJESTY!
I'VE BEEN PATIENT FOR TWO YEARS!
I FEAR FOR OUR COUNTRY, JOHN. I FEAR FOR THE CHURCH!
HE IS RIGHT; THIS IS ALL VERY TROUBLING INDEED.

A FEW MONTHS LATER, IN THE DEAD OF NIGHT ...
PIETRO, IT IS TIME ... TELL THE CONCLAVE THEY MUST ELECT A POPE WITHIN THE NEXT FOUR MONTHS!
YES, LORD! I WILL DO AS YOU ASK. I WILL TELL THE CARDINALS IMMEDIATELY.
OFFICE OF CARDINAL ORSINI.
HOW DID IT COME TO THIS? TWO YEARS AND NO ELECTION! MAY GOD GIVE US GUIDANCE ...
I HAVE NEWS, CARDINAL ORSINI.
WHAT IS IT, BROTHER?
DO YOU REMEMBER PIETRO DI MURRONE?
PIETRO DI MURRONE ...
OF COURSE!

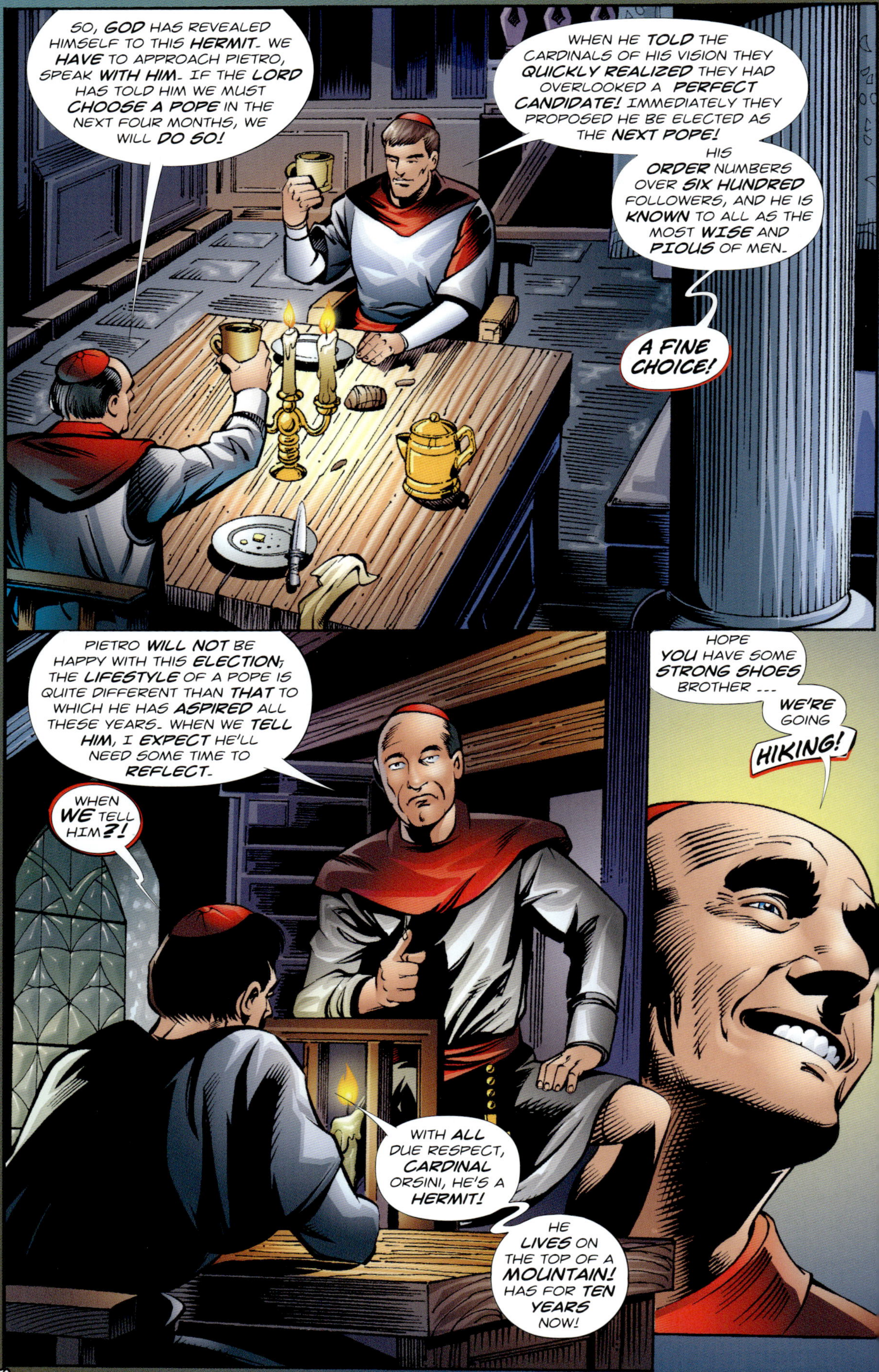

SO, GOD HAS REVEALED HIMSELF TO THIS HERMIT. WE HAVE TO APPROACH PIETRO, SPEAK WITH HIM. IF THE LORD HAS TOLD HIM WE MUST CHOOSE A POPE IN THE NEXT FOUR MONTHS, WE WILL DO SO!
WHEN HE TOLD THE CARDINALS OF HIS VISION THEY QUICKLY REALIZED THEY HAD OVERLOOKED A PERFECT CANDIDATE! IMMEDIATELY THEY PROPOSED HE BE ELECTED AS THE NEXT POPE!
HIS ORDER NUMBERS OVER SIX HUNDRED FOLLOWERS, AND HE IS KNOWN TO ALL AS THE MOST WISE AND PIOUS OF MEN.
A FINE CHOICE!
PIETRO WILL NOT BE HAPPY WITH THIS ELECTION; THE LIFESTYLE OF A POPE IS QUITE DIFFERENT THAN THAT TO WHICH HE HAS ASPIRED ALL THESE YEARS. WHEN WE TELL HIM, I EXPECT HE'LL NEED SOME TIME TO REFLECT.
WHEN WE TELL HIM?!
WITH ALL DUE RESPECT, CARDINAL ORSINI, HE'S A HERMIT!
HE LIVES ON THE TOP OF A MOUNTAIN! HAS FOR TEN YEARS NOW!
HOPE YOU HAVE SOME STRONG SHOES BROTHER ...
WE'RE GOING
HIKING!

A FEW DAYS LATER --- THE MOUNTAINS OF MURRONE.
WHY DO THE CLOUDS LOOK SO OMINOUS TODAY? IS IT A SIGN?
NO, IT'S PROBABLY NOTHING ---
DEAREST LORD, MY CREATOR! BRING ME COMFORT, I –
KRAK
SNAP
CRASH!
WHA–?
WHO'S THERE?!

PIETRO! THERE YOU ARE!
CARDINAL ORSINI. I TRUST YOU HAVE HEARD WHAT THE LORD HAS REVEALED TO ME.
YOU ARE OBVIOUSLY IN TUNE WITH THE HOLY SPIRIT!
YOUR VISION HAS MOVED US GREATLY, BROTHER. THAT IS WHY SO MANY OF US HAVE COME TO SPEAK WITH YOU.
I AM A PRIVATE MAN.
WHILE I APPRECIATE YOUR EFFORTS,
IT REALLY WAS NOT NECESSARY FOR YOU TO TRAVEL SO FAR.
WE HAVEN'T COME JUST TO VISIT WITH YOU, BROTHER PIETRO.

WHERE IS HE GOING?
HE NEEDS TIME ALONE, TO PRAY AND REFLECT.
THESE WOODS ARE HIS LIFE. CAN YOU IMAGINE GOING FROM THIS TO BECOMING THE POPE?
LORD, MY WHOLE LIFE I HAVE LIVED TO SERVE YOU AND YOU ALONE ...
BUT ME? THE POPE?
TRUST ME, PIETRO; I WILL GIVE YOU THE STRENGTH YOU NEED.
THOUGH MY HEART DOUBTS, I CHOOSE TO FOLLOW YOU. YOUR WILL, NOT MINE BE DONE.

BROTHER PIETRO?
WILL HE ACCEPT?!
PLEASE, TELL US YOUR DECISION, BROTHER!
I AM HONORED TO ACCEPT.
THIS IS A DAY OF CELEBRATION!
YOU ARE TRULY A GREAT MAN, PIETRO.
BUT WHAT KIND OF POPE WILL I BE?
FATHER, THIS TASK SEEMS LOFTY FOR ONE SUCH AS MYSELF, BUT I PUT MY TRUST IN YOU.
GRANT ME PEACE... GUIDE ME BY YOUR SPIRIT.

FROM THE MONASTERIES TO THE CASTLE, WORD OF PIETRO'S DECISION SPREAD QUICKLY ACROSS ITALY.
AT LAST! THE LORD HAS HEARD OUR PRAYERS.
BUT A HUMBLE MONK NOW POPE?
QUICKLY! WE MAKE FOR AQUILA TODAY! I MUST HONOR THE NEW POPE!
NOW WE CAN FINALLY GET THINGS MOVING!
CARDINAL GAETANI! KING CHARLES II OF NAPLES HAS CALLED THE SACRED COLLEGE TO AQUILA. PIETRO DI MURRONE HAS ACCEPTED! SHALL I GET THE HORSES?
YES, WE'LL LEAVE IMMEDIATELY.
WHY DO I HAVE SUCH A BAD FEELING ABOUT THIS?

THE YEAR 1294. AQUILA, ITALY. FIRST CROWNING OF POPE CELESTINE V, FORMERLY KNOWN AS PIETRO DI MURRONE, BELOVED HERMIT AND FOUNDER OF THE ORDER OF BENEDICTINE CELESTINES.
LORD, PLEASE GUIDE ME.
PLEASE GIVE ME WISDOM, DIRECTION, AND PEACE.
YOUR HOLINESS, WE MUST BEGIN THE CROWNING.
HAS EVERYONE ARRIVED?
DON'T WORRY YOURSELF!
THE CARDINALS WILL BE HERE SHORTLY...
TRUST ME.
DEAREST FATHER, THY WILL BE DONE.

AFTER THE CROWNING ...
A TERRIBLE MISTAKE!
CARDINAL ORSINI --
TO CROWN THE POPE WITHOUT ALL CARDINALS PRESENT AND ACCOUNTED FOR?! HOW COULD THIS HAPPEN?
PLEASE, CALM DOWN. YOUR HEALTH ...
MY HEALTH? WHAT MATTERS OF MY HEALTH, BROTHER?
I SHOULD HAVE KNOWN!
WE SHOULD HAVE NEVER ...
PLEASE LEAVE ME! I MUST PRAY.
YES ... OF COURSE.
FATHER IN HEAVEN ... HELP US.

DECEMBER 13, 1294: FIVE MONTHS INTO HIS PAPACY.
I HAVE DONE AS YOU HAVE ASKED, YOUR MAJESTY. I FEAR I DO NOT ENTIRELY UNDERSTAND WHY IT IS NECESSARY ...
YOUR HOLINESS, THANK YOU.
I WILL NOT BOTHER YOU WITH THE COMPLEXITIES OF POLITICS AND GOVERNMENT. YOU HAVE MORE IMPORTANT MATTERS TO ATTEND TO, AND I MUST BE ON MY WAY!!
THAT'S JUST THE THING! SO MANY MATTERS TO ATTEND TO, AND I DON'T KNOW HALF OF WHAT THEY MEAN!
LORD, SHOULD I HAVE REFUSED THIS ELECTION?
BUT HOW COULD I FORSAKE THE NEEDS OF THE CARDINALS, OF THE CHURCH?
PIETRO, HAVE FAITH. THIS SEASON IS DRAWING TO A CLOSE. FEAR NOT, FOR I AM WITH YOU ALWAYS.

POPE CELESTINE, THERE HE IS!
I MUST TELL HIM OF THE CORRUPTION AMONG THE OFFICIALS IN NAPLES.
SINCE HIS CROWNING, MULTIPLE MEN ARE CLAIMING ONE POSITION, DECREES ARE CONTRADICTING EACH OTHER ---
I MUST SPEAK TO HIM --- AT ONCE!
YOUR HOLINESS, I HAVE GRAVE NEWS --
STOP!
PLEASE ---
I'M SORRY, CARDINAL GAETANI. PLEASE, GATHER THE CARDINALS. I NEED TO SPEAK WITH EVERYONE AS SOON AS POSSIBLE.
RIGHT AWAY, YOUR HOLINESS.

CARDINALS, FOR THE PAST FIVE MONTHS I HAVE STRUGGLED TO SERVE THE CHURCH AND MY LORD AS POPE.
I HAVE MADE DECREES, I HAVE TRAVELED ACROSS THE COUNTRY, I HAVE PRAYED, AND I HAVE APPOINTED MANY OF YOU TO THE POSITIONS YOU HOLD TODAY.
YOU ALL KNOW THAT I AM BUT A HUMBLE HERMIT; I HAVE LONGED ONLY TO SERVE THE LORD WITH MY LIFE, BUT IN THE LAST FIVE MONTHS I FEAR I MAY HAVE CAUSED MORE DAMAGE THAN GOOD.
THE LORD HAS ANSWERED MY PRAYERS AND GIVEN ME PEACE. I MUST RESIGN AS YOUR POPE, AND RETURN TO MY LIFE AS A MONK.
YES LORD, IT IS TIME.
AS I RETURN TO THE MOUNTAINS OF MURRONE ---
BE WITH THESE BROTHERS ---
HELP THEM TO UNDERSTAND.

THE CONCLAVE GATHERED TO ELECT ANOTHER POPE.
IN CONTRAST TO THE TWO YEARS IT TOOK TO ELECT POPE CELESTINE V, THE CONCLAVE MADE A SWIFT DECISION AND APPOINTED CARDINAL GAETANI, WHO TOOK THE NAME POPE BONIFACE VIII.
YOU SUMMONED US, POPE BONIFACE?
I SENSE UNREST AMONG THE CARDINALS AND THE PEOPLE. KING CHARLES'S OPPOSITION TO CELESTINE'S RESIGNATION AND THE MANY PROTESTS COULD THREATEN THE UNITY OF THE CHURCH.
WHY WOULD THEY PROTEST HIS RESIGNATION? I AM THE POPE NOW! HE MUST BE HIDDEN OUT OF SIGHT!
I DO NOT WISH TO WORRY ABOUT CELESTINE ANY LONGER!
YOUR HOLINESS, WHAT IS IT YOU DESIRE US TO DO?
ARE YOU FAMILIAR WITH
THE CASTLE OF FUMONE?

AND HERE I AM.
EVEN IN THE MOUNTAINS, SO REMOVED FROM ALL OTHER MEN, I WAS NEVER ALONE.
YOU WERE ALWAYS WITH ME, LORD, IN THE MOUNTAINS, IN THE PALACE, AND NOW IN THIS TOWER.
IT'S STRANGE HOW SOME THINGS DON'T WORK OUT, LORD ---
AND IT'S COMFORTING HOW SOME THINGS DO.
SOON, LORD, I'LL JOIN YOU ON THAT MOUNTAIN MOST HIGH.
POPE ST. CELESTINE V WAS CANONIZED BY POPE CLEMENT V IN 1313 FOR HIS HUMBLE, LIFELONG SERVICE TO THE ORDER OF THE BENEDICTINE CELESTINES AND TO THE LORD.
THE CASTLE OF FUMONE STILL CELEBRATES HIS DEATH EVERY YEAR WITH A FUNERAL SERVICE.
MILLIONS OF VISITORS TO THE SMALL ITALIAN LANDMARK CAN VIEW THE CELL WHERE THIS SAINT SPENT THE LAST MONTHS OF HIS LIFE.
HE PASSED AWAY IN MAY 1296.

A Saint's Journey

✝ **1215:** Pietro di Murrone is born into a peasant family in south-central Italy. At a young age, he shows great intelligence and sensitivity. As a teenager, Pietro becomes a Benedictine monk.

✝ **c.1235:** Pietro begins living in solitude in the Apennine Mountains. Like many great hermits and ascetics, he attracts many visitors, despite his desire for privacy. These would-be followers convince him to go to Rome to be ordained a priest.

✝ **1246:** After receiving Holy Orders, Pietro resumes his solitary life in the Apennines. His persistent admirers eventually form a monastic community under the Benedictine rule, with Pietro as their head. The community forms close ties with a group of Franciscans.

✝ **1264:** Pope Urban IV grants official approval to Pietro's order, later known as the Celestines.

✝ **1274:** Pietro again leaves the mountains, this time for France. Pope Gregory X had convened the Second Council of Lyon to consider, among other reforms, the suppression of new religious orders. Pietro persuades the pope to approve his order as a branch of the Benedictines.

✝ **1292:** After Pope Nicholas IV's death, the College of Cardinals splits into two factions, each backing a powerful family. The infighting prolongs the election for two years.

✝ **1294:** Pietro writes a letter to the cardinals warning them of divine vengeance should they fail to elect a pope. The college then unanimously elects Pietro, and a group of dignitaries climb up the mountain to fetch him. In tears and with great reluctance, Pietro accepts the papacy and takes the name Celestine V. Because King Charles II of Naples rushes the first papal coronation, Celestine has to be crowned again.

During the five months of his papacy, Celestine struggles to maintain order and commits a series of blunders. King Charles and the cardinals take advantage of the new pope's naïveté.

Finally, Pope Celestine resigns the papacy on December 13,1294.The College of Cardinals elects Cardinal Benedetto Gaetani, who takes the name Boniface VIII. The new pope has Celestine imprisoned in the castle of Fumone.

✝ **1296:** On May 19, Celestine dies.

✝ **1313:** Pope Clement V canonizes Celestine.

When is the right time to accept God's protection?

SAINT
CLARE OF ASSISI
joe

SAINT CLARE OF ASSISI

It is said she conquered an army with a ***single prayer.***

It is known she was a woman of ***great spirit,*** strength, and intelligence. St. Clare, beloved abbess of the ***Order of Poor Ladies***, will remain a model of faith, ***courage, and passion*** for the Lord.

St. Clare of Assisi's life is ***rich and vibrant***, a testimony to her unique and ***unconquerable strength*** of character and faith. Born to a life of nobility, young Clare left her home behind to join St. Francis of Assisi, continuing on to lead her followers, known as the ***Poor Clares***, in a life of sacrifice and ministry. St. Clare ***trusted unfailingly*** in the Lord to provide her and her community all of their needs, focusing her energies on ***spreading the word of the Lord*** and putting His ***teachings into action.***

Greatly ***respected*** in her time by St. Francis of Assisi and his brothers, St. Clare was known for her ***compassionate heart*** and her ***attitude of humble service.*** She was always ***attentive*** to the ***needs*** of those around her, often forsaking her own well-being for that of another.

Her story ***inspires*** us to this day to ***follow our hearts***, for with faith, they will ***lead*** us to the Lord.

Producer: Daniel Burton

Editorial: Kimberly Black

Story: Jen Murvin Edwards

Pencils: Joe Dodd

Letters & Designs: Keith Bahrenburg

Inks: Justin Holman

Colors: Daniel Burton

Assisi, Italy. 1244
This night brings more than darkness to the lands of Assisi.
Emperor Frederick's forces have struck like a snake in the grass.
Sister Clare, the soldiers approach San Damiano ... they have agreed to your request.
I fear for San Damiano.
So it will be done.
I fear for my sisters.
I fear, Lord, for Assisi.
Where is she?
Sister Clare is ready, Captain.
Once more, I am asked to show courage, here, in my homeland.
Once more, I will take a stand for the Lord ...

Assisi, Italy. 1212. Thirty-Two Years Earlier.
I was only a young woman, and yet it seems like just yesterday ...
Clare ... Clare!
Mother? I'm sorry, I --
What has filled your ears, daughter, that you have not heard me calling out your name?
My own thoughts are to blame.
A woman's thoughts must be of her duties: her family, her husband. As you possess neither, I wonder what is left to occupy your mind so pervasively.
For what is a life, after all, when a woman is simply a woman.
I wonder what you will say, Mother, when I tell you now that I converse with my Lord.

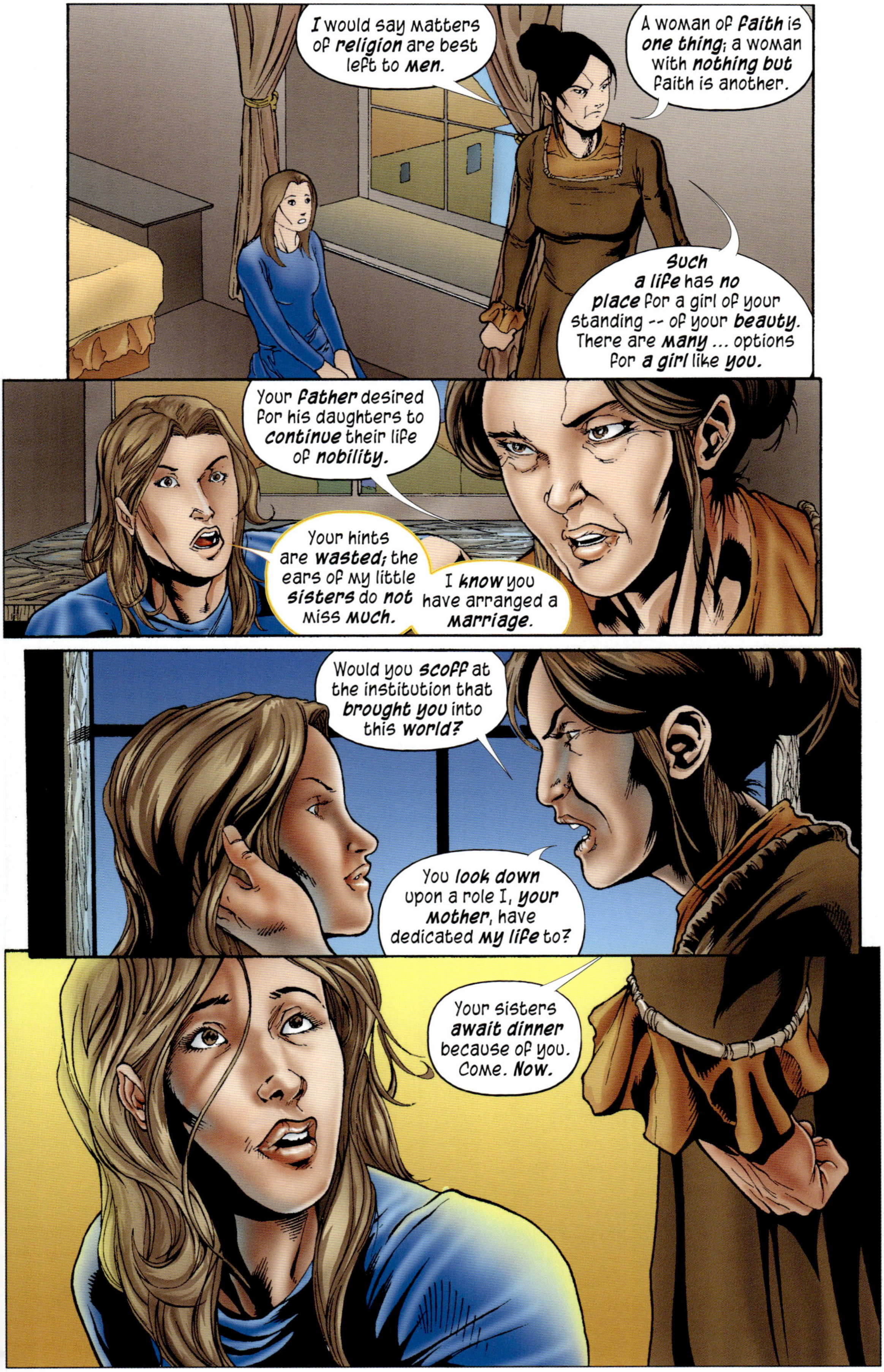
I would say matters of religion are best left to men.
A woman of faith is one thing; a woman with nothing but faith is another.
Such a life has no place for a girl of your standing -- of your beauty. There are many ... options for a girl like you.
Your father desired for his daughters to continue their life of nobility.
Your hints are wasted; the ears of my little sisters do not miss much.
I know you have arranged a marriage.
Would you scoff at the institution that brought you into this world?
You look down upon a role I, your mother, have dedicated my life to?
Your sisters await dinner because of you. Come. Now.

Palm Sunday. Cathedral of Assisi.
The blessing of palms. It is a much-loved tradition.
But even in the midst of this celebration, my heart was heavy.
Clare, you're so pale ...
What is happening? Shall I --
Caterina and Beatrice, I am well. Do not worry -- I simply have much on my mind. Let us pray.
The Bible tells of the dove who, at the end of the floods, brought an olive branch to Noah's ark. I could only imagine the joy felt by all as their eyes drank in the sight of that olive branch.
The dove's olive branch was a symbol of a new beginning -- a symbol of the Lord's great love and mercy.
The branches signify victory over death, the advent of spiritual anointment through Christ.
And yet, I could not bring myself to stand.
Yes -- the olive branch was a symbol of a new beginning.

My burden has been lifted, for I know now that my only life is with the Lord.
May my family forgive me, for I must travel in secret ...
And I will not return.

I have found none who know of her whereabouts --
It is certain -- Clare has fled!
If you know where your sister went -- you must tell me -- where is my daughter?
Is she alright?! Caterina, is she safe?! Please --
Signora di Fiumi! Signora --
I have heard -- Assisi has heard!
Your Clare -- she has fled to the community of Francis of Assisi, the holy preacher. She has been delivered to the convent of St. Paul.

Shall I summon your relations, Signora?
I would be grateful for it, thank you.
Mother, for what purpose would you summon the family?
Mother!
What is it you plan to do?
I'm scared. Is Clare alright? Please tell me what has happened.
Hush, darling Beatrice. Our sister has a chosen a life of faith, to become a nun.
She has chosen to be married to the Lord.
She has joined Francis -- the man of God we heard speak in San Giorgio.
It is already decided. We will travel to Bastia, to the convent of St. Paul. Our relations will accompany us. Their presence will bring us strength for our task.
We will be bringing your sister home.

Bastia, Italy. Convent of St. Paul.
CLARE!
This -- ridiculousness -- will stop at once! Do you hear me?! I am your mother!
Mother! What are you doing here?
God, strengthen me.
My life is no longer yours, Mother, nor mine.
What have you done?

You are to be WED!
!
GASP!
?
I have pledged my life to Christ.
I will have no other husband.
I am happy, Mother.
The more you continue to persecute me, the more God strengthens me. With His aid, I will overcome your efforts to remove me from the life I have chosen, the life He has chosen for me.
Please, leave me to the Lord's work.

Assisi, Italy. 1244
In our pain, You healed us, Lord, as only You can.
Not long after, both Mother and Caterina joined me at San Damiano. Due to her new state in life, Caterina changed her name to Agnes.
Give me strength now, Lord, as You did then...
...for an even greater struggle lies ahead this night.
Sister, I will perform my duty and escort you to the wall, but I must warn you...
...Surely your eyes are too holy to witness evidence of a soldier's sacrifice.
The battle has yet to cease.
I have seen death, Captain. I have seen it snatch children from my arms.
No, I am not afraid to see death. Now please, I must have silence.
I must prepare to petition my Lord.

This wall protects Assisi from its enemies.
But tonight, Assisi is in need of more. Much more.
But Sister Clare, you will be in full view of the enemy.
And that, my child ...
... is the very point.
It is time.

Lord, help us.

Does it please Thee, O God, to deliver into the hands of these beasts the defenseless children whom I have nourished with Thy love?*
*Actual words of St. Clare as written in Butler's "Lives of the Saints."

I will always have them in my care.*
* Actual response as reported in Butler's "Lives of the Saints."
NOOOOO!
What miracle do I see before my eyes?!

Lord, I *pray* for Assisi, for its *lands* and its *countrymen.*
Protect them ...
... as only You can.
Be assured.
I will always have them in my care.

Have no fear, little daughters; trust in Jesus.*
*Actual words of St. Clare as written in Butler's "Lives of the Saints."
My sisters -- please take me home...
...home to San Damiano.
Once again, Lord, You have delivered me.
Once again, Lord, You have shown Your great mercy.

The emperor's heart is stained with greed.
In defiance of these miraculous events, he has yet again laid siege to Assisi.
Poverty, chastity, obedience. We deny all worldly possessions, all worldly ambitions. We do so to honor You, Lord, to love You that much more fully.
Through the people of Assisi, You provide us with all our needs. I am never fearful, for You are my provider.
We pray once again for deliverance, Lord.

One Day Later.
Word arrives! The Lord has triumphed -- the enemy flees!
Agnes, my dear sister, your news cheers my heart more than I can say.
The soldiers have seen it with their own eyes.
It is as before -- the enemy has taken their leave.
With His strength, anything is possible.
I have never doubted Him...
...as I have never doubted my big sister -- even when she tricked me into mischief as a child.
Me? I do not know what you mean.
Come, Agnes, for once again the Lord has given us a new beginning.
Let us see what we make of it, shall we?
"Go forth in peace, for you have followed the good road. Go forward without fear, for He that created you has sanctified you, has always protected you, and loves you as a mother. Blessed be Thou, O God."
~ St. Clare of Assisi

A Saint's Journey

1193: ***St. Clare*** is born to Ortolana di Fiumi and Faverone Offreduccio. She is the eldest of three sisters, the others being ***Agnes*** (born Caterina) and, lastly, ***Beatrice.***

1210: St. Clare travels to hear ***St. Francis*** preach at the church of San Giorgio in Assisi. She later spoke with him of her desire to follow the Lord. ***St. Francis*** offered her his wisdom concerning the love of God and contempt for the world.

1212: On Palm Sunday, St. Clare attends the ***blessing of palms***; that evening she leaves home and arrives at the ***Portiuncula.*** They receive her in the chapel of ***Our Lady of the Angels***, where St. Francis cuts St. Clare's hair and outfits her with his penitential habit.

St. Clare is sent to live in the Benedictine convent of ***St. Paul*** in the absence of a Franciscan nunnery.

After the failed attempt of St. Clare's relatives to remove her from her new life, St. Clare is moved to the nunnery of ***Sant'Angelo di Panzo.***

St. Clare's younger sister, ***St. Agnes of Assisi***, joins St. Clare at the age of fifteen and is given the habit by St. Francis.

St. Clare and St. Agnes are placed at a poor house near the church of ***San Damiano.*** St. Clare becomes superior, and is soon joined by her mother and other ladies of the community.

Monasteries of her followers, known as the Poor Ladies or ***Poor Clares***, are established across Italy, France, and Germany. St. Clare and her followers practice a rigorous rejection of material wealth, sleeping on the ground and wearing no shoes, abstaining from meat and remaining silent, speaking only when ***absolutely necessary.*** So great is St. Clare's fasting that St. Francis and his brothers are obliged to ensure that she eat bread once a day for nourishment.

1244: It is said that St. Clare's prayer delivered Assisi from the siege of Emperor Frederick II's enemy forces.

The rule of the ***Poor Ladies*** is rewritten several times until a final rule is approved by Pope Innocent IV for the convent of San Damiano, two days before St. Clare's death.

1253: St. Clare begins a long, painful struggle with her health. She is visited twice by ***Pope Innocent IV.*** It is written that he wished he had as little need of absolution as St. Clare. She passes away peacefully among her brothers and sisters in the Faith.

1255: St. Clare is canonized by ***Pope Alexander IV.***

GO!
Make disciples of all nations.

Baptize them in the name of the Father, the Son, and the Holy Spirit.

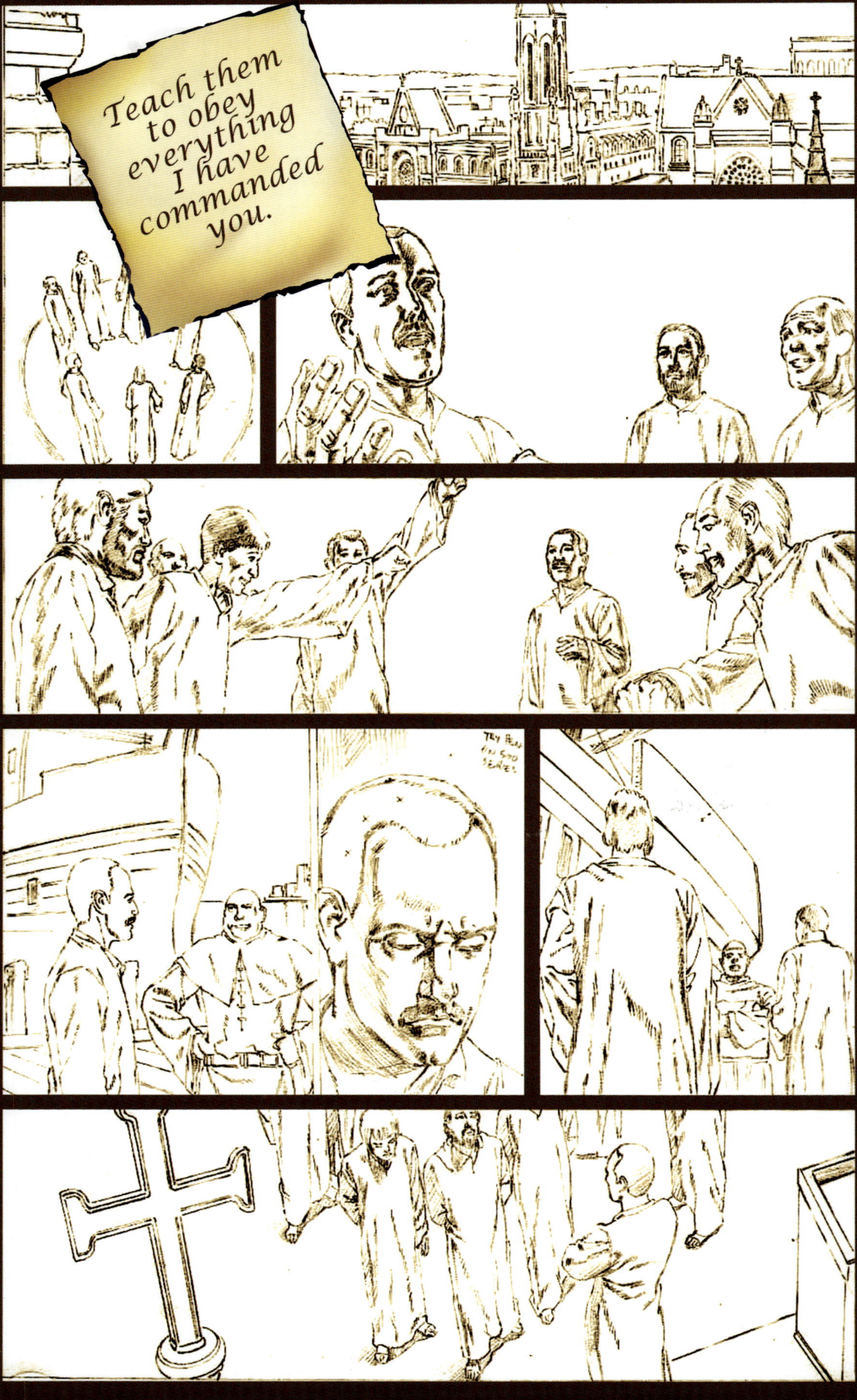
Teach them to obey everything I have commanded you.

Matthew
28:19-20a

*GO!

Make disciples of all nations.

Baptize them in the name of the Father, the Son, and the Holy Spirit.

Teach them to obey everything I have commanded you.

Matthew 28:19-20a